'Karen Webb's comprehensive but highly readable introductory work brings the Enneagram to life. Making excellent use of the self-observations of self-aware people, Webb leads readers straight into the wonders of this amazing system for understanding human personality. It is particularly useful for those who want to better understand their relationships with others. This book is a great introduction to those who are approaching the Enneagram as relative beginners.'

> — *Terry Saracino, MA, MBA, President of Enneagram Studies in the Narrative Tradition*

'Whatever its origins, the Enneagram has become an invaluable tool, in many walks of life, for growing emotional intelligence, enhancing self-awareness and social competence, and personal development. Karen Webb draws on a lifetime of study and practice to provide a comprehensive guide both for those who are new to the Enneagram and those who wish to go on exploring its value for understanding themselves and the many relationships which shape their lives. As only the true expert can, she brings to a complex subject the gift of clarity without in any way being simplistic. In accessible language she analyses and describes the nine different personality types in a way which is engaging and illuminating in equal measure.'

> — *Rt Revd Dr Michael Langrish, Bishop of Exeter*

'*Principles of the Enneagram* by Karen A. Webb is one of the most comprehensive and well-written books on the Enneagram. The language is simple, lucid and well expressed, and the book will satisfy all kinds of readers, from those who want a deeper understanding of the whole system to those who are interested in the related topics. The result of more than two decades' work, this book is timely, practical and constructive, and will help readers acquire a greater understanding of themselves and how they interact with others.'

*— Dr Satishchandra Kumar, Associate Professor,
Department of Applied Psychology and
Counselling, University of Mumbai, India*

'Still the only introduction you'll ever need and the best around. We gave copies to most of our clients, and we'll certainly let them know the revised version should be added to their shelves.'

— Peter Neall, Neall Scott Partnership

PRINCIPLES OF THE ENNEAGRAM
What it is, how it works, and
what it can do for you

other books in the series

Principles of Chinese Medicine

Angela Hicks
ISBN 978 1 84819 130 3
eISBN 978 0 85701 107 7

Principles of Chinese Herbal Medicine

John Hicks
ISBN 978 1 84819 133 4
eISBN 978 0 85701 107 7

PRINCIPLES OF

THE
ENNEAGRAM

2nd Edition

Karen A. Webb

FOREWORD BY HELEN PALMER

SINGING
DRAGON
LONDON AND PHILADELPHIA

This edition published in 2013
by Singing Dragon
an imprint of Jessica Kingsley Publishers
73 Collier Street
London N1 9BE, UK
and
400 Market Street, Suite 400
Philadelphia, PA 19106, USA

www.singingdragon.com

First edition published in 1996 by Thorsons, an imprint of HarperCollins

Copyright © Karen A. Webb 1996, 2013
Foreword copyright © Helen Palmer 1996, 2013

Printed digitally since 2016

The moral right of the author has been asserted.

Library of Congress Cataloging in Publication Data
Webb, Karen, 1951-
  Principles of the enneagram / Karen A. Webb.
    p. cm.
  "Revised Edition"--Pref.
  ISBN 978-1-84819-123-5 (alk. paper)
  1. Enneagram. 2. Typology (Psychology)--Religious aspects. I. Title.
  BF698.35.E54W43 2013
  155.2'6--dc23

British Library Cataloguing in Publication Data
A CIP catalogue record for this book is available from the British Library

ISBN 978 1 84819 123 5
eISBN 978 0 85701 099 5

CONTENTS

Foreword by Helen Palmer 9

ACKNOWLEDGEMENTS 11

PREFACE TO THE SECOND EDITION 13

Introduction: Why the Enneagram? 15

1 How the Enneagram Works 22

2 Type One: The Perfectionist 46

3 Type Two: The Giver 59

4 Type Three: The Performer 72

5 Type Four: The Romantic 85

6 Type Five: The Observer 98

7 Type Six: The Questioner 111

8 Type Seven: The Optimist 124

9 Type Eight: The Protector 137

10 Type Nine: The Mediator 150

11 Seeing Below the Surface: Types
That Look Alike 163

12 Communication: Using the
Enneagram to Create Understanding 180

Conclusion: What Do I Do Now? 196

FURTHER READING AND USEFUL CONTACTS 205

Foreword

I am delighted to support the revised edition of Karen Webb's *Principles of the Enneagram*, a book that remains in steady demand. Hers is a wise and popular introduction that especially pleases those of us who teach in the Narrative method of reporting our self-observations to others.

The whole point of discovering your Enneagram type is to strengthen self-observation. We must learn to mentally step back and witness our own mind at work. Only inner observation can help us to uncover type, because my type is who I think I am.

For many, self-observation is still a latent ability, but it can quickly become dependable by watching our habit of mind. Only I can witness the nuances of my own thinking, and only I can recognise when my passions arise.

It's the search and discovery mission that strengthens us spiritually, because we cannot move forward into the territory described as Essence without a reliable inner observer as a guide.

Karen Webb clearly describes the take-off point for the inward journey. We have to start somewhere in the quest to discover the Essence that lies beyond the limitations of type, and what better vantage point than a concise description of what can be called the Enneagram Ego-Essence equation?

Ms Webb gives us a clear encapsulation of the recurring habits that animate and limit different types of people. More than that, she has had the patience and good sense to listen to the ways in which different types of people describe this dilemma rather than imposing her own views on them.

It was with pleasure that in 1996 I welcomed her book to the emerging library of the Narrative Tradition, in which each of us describes the dilemma of seeing through our personality to the common Essence shared by all beings. It is with pleasure that I welcome this new edition.

Helen Palmer
Author of The Enneagram *(1991) and other works*
Berkeley, California, 2012

ACKNOWLEDGEMENTS

My gratitude and love always to Helen Palmer, whom I believe to be the foremost Enneagram teacher alive, and her co-teacher, David Daniels MD. Their Enneagram Professional Training Programs in the Narrative Tradition are so profound and inspiring that I keep going back, decades after graduating.

Deep thanks also to the hundreds of people (thousands, by the time of this new edition) who have allowed me to hear their stories, and heard mine with compassion. They have never withheld, placing wisdom, empathy and the shared humour of our human condition higher than maintaining face. In particular (in numerical order!): Jon Neall, Andy Kirkwood, Kate Nuttall, Ralph Rolls, Jeremy Walters, Steve Jorgensen, Patricia Miller, Nousheh Rahbari-Hodgson, Craig Orrock, Verena Tschudin, Lucinda Neall, Peter Neall, Simon Webb, Stephen Moorby, James Kirk, John Rees and the late Toby Falk, for their input to their chapters.

Finally, thanks to Simon for his patience and many ways of supporting me, and Peter for his lovingly constructive criticism.

PREFACE TO THE
SECOND EDITION

When, in 1994, I was invited by HarperCollins to write the first English book (as contrasted to American English) on the Enneagram, it was as part of their Thorsons Principles series. This series offered in-depth yet accessible introductions to a range of topics relating to health, growth and spirituality, ranging as far apart as colonic irrigation and Buddhism.

Their emphasis was on conciseness (I was given a word limit), thoroughness and clarity. The strap line on the front of each book was 'The Only Introduction You'll Ever Need'.

In revising the text for this edition I have actually changed very little, as I have been told again and again by my readers that it actually was the best introduction they had found. Gratifyingly, I'm still hearing this over a decade and a half after first publication. If it ain't broke, why fix it? Moreover, this is still an introduction and needs to stay clear and concise.

I've changed the names of Types Seven and Eight from Epicure and Boss to Optimist and Protector respectively, as I feel they're more representative.

With the word limit lifted, I have altered some phrases slightly where I felt a few more words were needed to really clarify the point. I've added a little more to the sections on subtypes, though not much because that is a book topic in itself! I've also expanded somewhat upon the 'spiritual gift' aspect of type – that's the part I'm most passionate about, and the part I regretted having to keep so short in the first edition.

Above all, however, I've applied the learning gained in nearly two decades since the first edition, of teaching and working with the Enneagram. Some of what I wrote back then was too simplistic, and whilst that word count had something to do with it, I know a lot more now.

And that's the message I'd like to pass on: the Enneagram offers a lifetime of learning, layer upon layer of deepening insight. Whenever I run a workshop, or work with a new individual, or catch my type in action yet again, I learn: about others, about myself. May you too find the Enneagram to be such a powerful resource.

Introduction

Why the Enneagram?

When, in 1990, I was asked by an enthusiastic friend to look at the Enneagram, my first thought (as a former management trainer) was: 'Not another personality system, please. No more boxes to put me in.' But within two days my initial reaction had turned to one of: 'Eureka! This is pure gold.' Far from pigeon-holing, it offered a map of the terrain I inhabited daily, together with signposts as to how to get *out* of the box that I, along with every other human being, was already in.

As a practising student of psychology and comparative religion for over 20 years at that time, I had found many valuable truths and many parallels, but one thing puzzled me. Whatever their methods, healers can agree on the symptoms of disease and what a healthy body looks like – so, surely, in the field of the psyche and spirit there must also be a universal definition of the 'healthy' being and its symptoms of unhealth, which we can agree on and work with in our different disciplines?

The Enneagram (from the Greek *enneas*, meaning nine, and *gramma*, meaning something written) solves this conundrum. It is an ancient and beautifully accurate description of human personality in all its diversity and of how personality is directly linked to each person's spiritual self.

Not a religion, it encapsulates and unites apparently different principles found in all major faiths. Now psychologists of various schools have found it corresponds uncannily closely to modern personality descriptions.

Simple, accurate and profound, it links, explains and puts in context disparate elements of myself and how I (and others) work, which have otherwise taken years to understand.

Whether beginner or experienced self-explorer, the Enneagram has a unique role to play in the life of anyone seeking psychological or spiritual development or looking to bridge the gap between them.

For anyone, at any stage of his or her journey, of whatever spiritual background or none, the Enneagram fosters:

- deeper insight into who we are, our potential and how to attain it

- self-directed growth *from* whatever level *to* whatever level we wish

- more harmonious and creative daily lives

- deeper empathy, compassion and more creative relationships, through:

  - seeing ourselves as others see us

  - seeing others as they see themselves, rather than through our projections and beliefs

- the realisation that we do not need to 'conquer' our personality, but befriend it, understand it and use it to help our growth

- understanding of how our personality is the key to our personal spiritual path, whatever our religious beliefs.

About this book

This is an introduction to the Enneagram. In it you will discover what the Enneagram of personality is and how it works; descriptions of the nine personality types, including how they vary and interact; some discussion of the higher aspects of each type; and, finally, suggestions as to how to use this knowledge.

Through reading it, if you are honest with yourself, you should uncover your own personality type, and, through that, more about yourself and how to apply this to your personal growth. You will start to recognise friends' and colleagues' types and learn how to communicate more effectively with them. Moreover, the more you learn about other types, the more you learn about yourself by contrast. It can be astonishing to realise how very different other types' world views and assumptions are!

A book like this can only contain 'thumbnail sketches', and I have had to omit many subtleties of each type. All the quotations are verbatim or slightly disguised statements by normal people of that type, and although everybody manifests their type differently – we are all unique – you will start to recognise yourself in the words of people like you.

The Narrative Tradition

Throughout the known history of the Enneagram (see below) it has been taught orally as a personal guide to growth. Since the early 1990s there have been many books, and latterly websites, written about it, yet it is from individuals' experience of themselves, and not from theories, no matter how elegant, that we discover what it truly means to be human. People learn best about themselves and others through active participation, exploring the significance of their own and each other's stories.

The current Narrative Tradition, pioneered by transpersonal psychologist Helen Palmer, is based upon workshops in which people who know their own type talk about themselves, and, through skilful exploration and dialogue, extend participants' – and often their own – understanding of that type.

Everything in this book has been verified orally through the self-observation and self-disclosure of thousands of people, illustrated in the quotations.

Summarised history of the Enneagram

The Enneagram's nine-pointed star is an ancient diagram, and not an arbitrary device, though no one knows its origin. It encapsulates the esoteric Laws of Three and of Seven (also called Octaves), is very like Pythagoras's ninth seal symbolising humanity, and some researchers link ancient stone circles with the mathematics of the Enneagram.

Study, and application, of the wisdom embodied in the Enneagram ranges far further and deeper than the simple description of personality traits. For example, the nine points and their linking lines relate to different states or processes and their connected flow in time, necessary to any creatively successful undertaking. The Nine and the Three are to be found in all major religions.

However, this book concerns only the Enneagram of Personality, a modern name for an ancient wisdom of which the following is known for certain.

Christian mystics of the Desert Father tradition, in the third and fourth centuries CE, worked with the concept of converting vice to virtue, using personality traits named in the Enneagram. Evagrius Ponticus named nine interruptions to the life of prayer, and mentioned a diagram relating to these, though this has not (yet) been found. The Lord's Prayer addresses the nine types in sequence. A conversion concept including the diagram and nine personality types has also been a cornerstone of Sufi ethical training for 1400 years. Anecdotally, a Russian friend of a friend was taught it secretly by his Georgian grandmother, as an oral tradition passed on to her in the same way.

In the 1920s G. I. Gurdjieff, a mystic and spiritual teacher, brought it to Europe. He claimed to have learnt it from Sufis in Afghanistan, and used it, as they did, as an esoteric wisdom known only to spiritual teachers to determine practices for their pupils. He taught movements related to the diagram, but not the personality descriptions, saying that individuals would not be able to discern their own type as it is the foundation for, and therefore hidden from, the personality. He simply said that there are nine 'chief features' of mankind, and that everyone has one of these as the organising principle of their 'false personality'.

It remained a secret teaching until the late 1960s, when Oscar Ichazo initiated an intense psycho-spiritual training at Arica in Chile incorporating much of the esoteric wisdom of the Enneagram. It was he who revealed the correct key words or 'passions' assigned to each of the nine points. Many now famous people attended this training and subsequently wrote about it, including John Lilly, Joseph Hart and Claudio Naranjo, a transpersonal psychologist.

Naranjo took the still fairly rudimentary knowledge to California where he started a series of workshops to explore and extend understanding of the personality types described by the diagram, using discussion with people who recognised their type. Helen Palmer, also a transpersonal psychologist, and Bob Ochs, a Jesuit priest, built upon the insights they gained there in 1970–1971 and continued to expand our understanding and teach it in their own fields, Palmer vastly extending Naranjo's concept of the Enneagram as 'self-analysis for the seeker' and adding the insight that type is not about behaviours but a subconscious focus of attention. Ochs shared the basics with fellow religious, who in turn passed it on within religious communities. From these sources the Enneagram has spread rapidly around the world as others learnt and then started to teach it.

Using this book

I have tried to structure each chapter as though I am answering questions as they might occur to you. The next chapter deals with the structure of the Enneagram in four main sub-headings:

- basic personality type

- the significance of the diagram

- the internal structure of type; how type is defined

- the Enneagram as a tool for psychological and spiritual growth.

This is followed by a series of chapters, each on one type, which, for ease of access, are in numerical order. Each follows this structure:

- what that personality appears to be, and its extremes

- the habits of mind and concerns underlying that

- how that type changes in security and stress

- relationship issues

- practices for personal growth

- how friends can support growth

- the higher aspects of that type.

There is then a chapter on distinguishing between personalities that appear similar (look-alikes), one on creating greater understanding between types through communication, and finally some suggestions as to where to go from here.

First, then, is the task of finding yourself in these pages. Once you have recognised your basic type, the one that runs like a hidden thread through your life, there is an 'Aha!' about it. There may even be a sense of relief, and some rueful discomfort. Sometimes there is also an 'Oh *no*, that's the one I didn't want to be!' When you are first looking for your type, don't discount one because it doesn't fit the kind of person you would like to be or think of yourself as: that may be just the type to examine more closely.

Some people will prefer to read the whole book through before trying to identify their type; others will find it more interesting and personal to follow the outline below. Either works well, so do what seems best to you.

The important thing to bear in mind is that it is not patterns of behaviour that determine type so much as the underlying focus of attention that motivates behaviour.

- Read Chapter 1 to understand how the Enneagram works.

- Scan the personality synopses for types you think you might be.

- Read the appropriate chapter(s).

- Observe yourself in action before you decide, bearing in mind that we all have blind spots based on what we would *like* to be.

- If you are unsure, refer to the chapter on look-alikes.

- Re-read Chapter 1 for deeper understanding of the subtleties of your (and others') type.

- Read Chapter 12: Communication.

- Follow the suggestions for further action and see what happens.

When trying to 'type' others, follow the same scan-and-check process – and refer to them, since they know themselves better than you do.

For a deeper understanding of the whole system, read the book through, referring to the diagrams, relating what you read to your own and others' lives. You may be surprised by what you discover.

Chapter 1

How the Enneagram Works

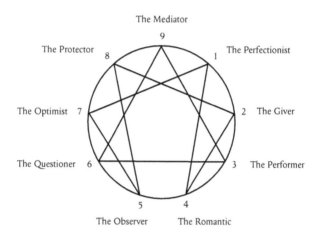

We are all unique. The Enneagram describes nine personality types, none better or worse than another, yet recognisably and radically different in their way of responding to the world. There are over seven billion of us on the planet – about three-quarters of a billion of each type; yet we *are* unique, and the Enneagram allows us to be so. Our personality *type* is identifiable and shared with others, but the way we manifest it, our personality – the experiences, memories, dreams and aspirations, and what we do with them – is our own.

This book deals mainly with the psychological aspects of type. Though the Enneagram describes aspects of higher awareness specific to each type (and this is where the real power of the system lies), we have to start with the obvious. We can all recognise ourselves at this level: we all deal with our personalities every day. This is where the work of knowing ourselves and understanding others begins.

All nine types are simply strategies for survival, all work well in their own way, and none is nicer, wiser and more ethical, nor more hateful or dysfunctional, than any other.

Moreover, the Enneagram is not prescriptive. It simply offers a description, a map, of the shape of each type's personality structure, good and bad, weaknesses and gifts, and of our highest self – it is then up to us how we use these insights. After all, the map is not the territory – and, if we're on a journey, it certainly helps.

The Enneagram model offers subtle layers of insight. The shape of the diagram is central to this. Each person inhabits one basic type, which does not change. However, the lines connecting the points show how each type changes in extreme stress and in emotional security (and allow us to predict how the nine personality types interact positively and negatively), whilst the external circle may bring in a flavour of the types on either side. Each type also has three distinct variants or subtypes.

All of this, together with our environment as children and our individual level of self-knowledge, means that two people may be of the same Enneagram type and yet appear very different – even opposite – in character.

For clarity's sake, then, this chapter on 'How the Enneagram Works' is in four sections:

- basic personality type, which includes thumbnail sketches of each of the types

- the diagram's structure: how it affects type and type interactions

- each type's structure, which describes the mental, emotional and instinctive elements of each type, both psychological and spiritual

- psychological and spiritual growth.

How the Enneagram works:
Basic personality type

It is now common knowledge that everyone filters, and unconsciously interprets, what they perceive. Indeed, some neuroscientists are now proposing that only 10 per cent of 'reality' – what could be perceived in any given moment – actually gets through to the conscious mind.

The basic principle of the Enneagram is that:

- each of us has adopted one of nine possible 'filters' which sets the tenor of our whole life, a habitual focus of attention so deep it is usually hidden from conscious awareness, *and*

- this filter was not developed at random, but to protect a specific aspect of our Essence (higher, or divine, self) that was particularly vulnerable in the infant self.

Although our personality developed as a strategy to help us cope with the outer world as infants, by the time we are adult it is an automatic biased perspective. The way we view others and interpret events is coloured by it; our choices and actions are usually, unconsciously, based on it.

The unique and heartening aspect of the Enneagram theory is that this 'false' or acquired personality reflects, as in a mirror image, our highest self. It is not an enemy to be conquered but our best friend, showing us which lessons we need to learn and how to learn them, and, even more significant, our innate gifts and how to nurture them.

Synopsis of types

The names for the types vary between teachers. They are simply shorthand ways of describing the overall personality. Some people prefer to refer to the types by number; others find that impersonal, and so names are given.

These are snapshots, not comprehensive or even universal descriptions, of the nine basic personality styles. The later sections show how these vary in different life circumstances, and other influences that affect how individuals express their type. The true definer of type is not found in behaviour, but in the unconscious focus of attention.

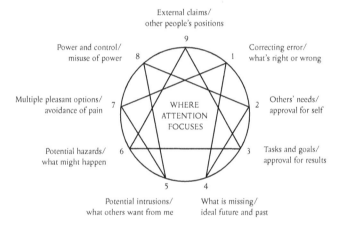

TYPE ONE: THE PERFECTIONIST

Critical of themselves and others, Type Ones have an internal list of shoulds and should nots. They take responsibility seriously and wish whatever they do to be done absolutely correctly. They find it difficult to allow themselves pleasure for its own sake, as they monitor their behaviour against very high standards and feel there is always more to do. They may procrastinate for fear of not 'getting it perfect'. Often feeling morally superior, Type Ones may also be resentful of others who don't follow the rules, especially if they seem to get away with it. Excellent organisers, they can spot just what's wrong and what needs to be done to get it right.

TYPE TWO: THE GIVER

Type Twos are active, helpful, generally optimistic and generous with time, energy and things. Since they do not find it easy to recognise their own needs or ask for help, they are unconsciously drawn to having their needs met through relationships, seeking approval through meeting others' needs, and are often happiest when indispensable. Very sensitive to others' needs and feelings, they are able to show just that part of their personality that will draw a person to them. Better at giving than receiving, they can at times be manipulative, giving to get, and at others genuinely caring and supportive. With their natural empathy, Type Twos are able to give what is truly needed for another's success and well-being.

TYPE THREE: THE PERFORMER

High-energy workaholics, Type Threes strive for success to gain status and approval. They are competitive, though view it as loving challenge more than a desire to beat others. Aiming to succeed in whatever arena they are in – the successful parent, spouse, businessperson, playmate, hippy, therapist – they change their image to suit the people they are with. Though out of touch with their real feelings as these interfere with achievement, they can display appropriate feelings if called for as part of the image. Type Threes are tireless and single-minded in pursuit of a goal. They make excellent team leaders, motivating others to believe anything is achievable.

Type Four: The Romantic

Artistic, passionate and searching for the ideal partner or life's work, Type Fours live with a sense of something essential missing in their lives. Feeling they would be complete if they could find true partnership, they tend to idealise the distant, the past and the future, and find fault with the available and mundane. Abandonment seems a fact of life, and this fear may lead them into a push–pull style of relating. They are drawn to the heights and depths of emotional experience, and to expressing themselves as unique and authentic. In whatever field, their lives reflect a search for the significant and meaningful. Though easily caught up in their own emotions, they can be supremely empathic with and supportive of others in emotionally painful situations.

Type Five: The Observer

Avoiding emotional involvement, Type Fives experience life from a distance, observing rather than engaging. They are private people, and may feel drained and anxious if not allowed sufficient time to themselves, which they use to review events, and to experience in safety emotions they do not feel whilst in the thick of things. The life of the mind is very important to them, and they have a love of knowledge and information, often quite specialised. Type Fives compartmentalise their lives with little or no overlap between areas of activity or groups of friends or colleagues, and, though they do not like predictable routine, like to know in advance what is expected of them both in work and leisure. They can be excellent decision makers and creative intellectuals.

Type Six: The Questioner

Though possibly unaware of being fearful, Type Sixes view the world as threatening. They scan for sources of threat and imagine worst possible outcomes, in order to be forearmed. Their doubting frame of mind may produce procrastination (do I have enough information yet?) and suspicion of others' motives. They question or fear authority, align themselves with underdog causes and are not at ease in authority or with continued success. Some Type Sixes tend to withdraw and protect themselves from threat; others pre-empt it by going forward to confront it, and may appear quite aggressive. Having given their trust, Type Sixes are loyal and committed friends, team members and seconds-in-command: 'comrades in arms'.

Type Seven: The Optimist

Type Sevens are optimistic, energetic, charming and elusive. They have a Peter Pan quality, hating to feel trapped or coerced, and keep as many pleasant options open as possible. In an unpleasant situation they can mentally escape to enjoyable fantasies. Type Sevens are future-oriented and have an internal future map that includes everything they want to achieve or experience, updating it as new options arise. Their need to keep life pleasant leads to 'reframing' reality, in order to exclude negative emotions and potential blows to their self-image as upbeat and effective people. They enjoy new experiences, new people and new ideas, and can be creative networkers, synthesisers and theoreticians.

TYPE EIGHT: THE PROTECTOR

Assertive, passionate and sometimes aggressive, Type Eights often have an all-or-nothing approach to life. They know what they think, are concerned about justice and fairness, and are willing to fight for them. Often the leader, or fiercely independent, they can be very protective of friends and people in their care. Type Eights can be excessive in the pursuit of enjoyment, which may be anything from drinking with friends to deep intellectual discussion. Aware of where power lies, they will not let themselves be controlled by others and can be dominating to avoid being dominated. Introvert Eights may not be overtly assertive, yet still oppose injustice and do things their own way. Type Eights can use their power in loyal and tireless support of a worthy cause.

TYPE NINE: THE MEDIATOR

Type Nines are peacemakers. Excellent at understanding everyone else's point of view, they are not so good at knowing what they themselves think or want. They like life to be harmonious and comfortable, and will go along with others' agendas rather than create a conflict. However, they can be stubborn or passive-aggressive if pressurised. They are usually very active, with many interests, but put off their own highest priorities till the last minute. Easily distracted from the task in hand by an interruption or a side issue, they also tend to keep personal priorities and anger at bay with low-priority activities such as reading, hanging out with friends and watching videos. Type Nines make good arbitrators and negotiators, and can focus a team project.

How the Enneagram works:
The diagram's structure

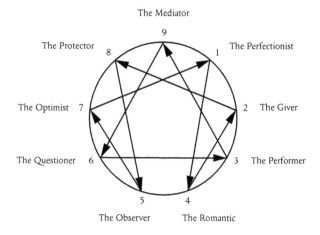

Whilst we all have one of the nine as our basic 'home' type, the diagram also shows each type's access along the lines to four others. Two of these, connected to us by arrows across the diagram, are givens. They are true for everyone of that type, and so constant that they are one of the ways to help determine which is your true type. The other two, on either side on the circle, and known as 'wings', are much less predictable.

Then there is the intriguing fact that, though a nine-pointed star, the diagram contains only one closed triangle: the 3–6–9. These are the central, or core, types in three triads (groups of three), which represent different basic ways of approaching the world.

The arrows: Stress and emotional security

Everybody's feelings and behaviour alter somewhat when they are under stress, and again when they are in an emotionally secure and positive life situation. The lines on the diagram show the shift in mental and emotional strategy that we experience in these circumstances. The direction of arrow indicates the change: for each type, the arrow points *towards* the stress point and *comes from* the security point.

It is important to note that stress and emotional security have many levels, and different degrees of these will have different results. For example, 'normal' stress, such as a hard day at work, will simply intensify basic type behaviour unless it continues. The move towards the stress type occurs when the stress is deep and pervasive. It can be described as an unconscious decision: 'Nothing I've tried to make this better has worked. No matter what I do, my strategies aren't working, so I'll try a different set.'

In similar vein, the word 'security' in this context does not mean material security or happy times when we're feeling good about life. The shift occurs when one is feeling *emotionally* secure – for example, in the first weeks or years of a loving relationship, or if we are appreciated and validated by a supportive boss. Nor is it necessarily a pleasant change; for example, Threes become fearful and Fours become perfectionistic. Once again, it is simply an unconscious shift in strategy because of life circumstances.

People do not 'become' another type in stress or security: they take on characteristics of that type, but retain the concerns and issues of their own type. If someone has been stressed or secure for a long time, they can appear very like their stress or security type, so when trying to identify type you may need to take life circumstances into account (see also Chapter 11 on look-alikes).

Although for most of us the word 'stress' has negative connotations, it is not in fact 'worse' to take on our stress point, nor is it 'better' to go towards our security type. Some types actually find it easier to be in stress than security, and some find the change they experience when emotionally secure very uncomfortable. It's not a question of feeling 'good' or 'bad', simply that we do change in predictable ways. Nor is it, as some people have suggested, less or more spiritually or psychologically healthy. In terms of growth, we can learn from both if we remember to focus on the positive qualities.

The wings

Each type has two 'wings' – the types on either side of it on the circle – and these may influence the way an individual manifests type. For example, a Type Six may at times lean towards Type Five and become more withdrawn, or towards Type Seven and become more playful.

There are several theories as to how the wings function in relation to type. In my experience, and from the evidence of 40 years of the Narrative Tradition teaching, wing influences seem to be particular to the individual – that is, they cannot be predicted. Looking at your own personality, you may find you 'lean' towards one wing or the other all the time, or to each at different times, or indeed to neither.

Start to explore wings only when you've determined your 'home' type.

The central triangle: Head, heart, belly

Human beings have three main ways of experiencing the world: thinking, feeling and sensing. The Enneagram model, and every mystical tradition, recognises three centres of perception and intelligence that mediate our life experiences and reactions to them, corresponding to the head, the heart and the belly.

Psychologically speaking, everyone uses all three centres (see next section). We all sense the environment, have emotional reactions and think about things, but each type favours one of them as their main channel for perceiving and responding to events. The diagram divides into three triads, each corresponding to one of the centres, and the types within are known as head, heart and belly types.

Each centre has its particular way of experiencing life, as well as the 'negative' emotion and concerns associated with it. The three types within each triad are the ones that favour that centre and reveal different ways of dealing with those specific issues.

The head centre is where we do our thinking: analysing, remembering, projecting ideas about other people and events, and planning future actions.

Head-based types (5, 6, 7) tend to respond to life through their thoughts. They have vivid imaginations and a strong ability to analyse and correlate ideas. Even the most gregarious of them say they can be completely satisfied with the company of their own thoughts. For these types, thinking is (usually unconsciously) a way of pre-empting fear in a potentially threatening world.

The heart centre is where we experience emotions: the wordless sensations that tell us how we feel rather than what we think about something. Emotions of the heart range from the strong and dramatic to the most subtle, almost muted, feelings. We feel connected to others in this centre, but also a yearning for love and fulfilment.

Heart-based types (2, 3, 4) operate in the world through relationship and are sometimes called 'image types' because they are concerned with how others see and relate to them. They are quick to sense another's needs or moods and respond to them, consciously or unconsciously. Successful relationships keep at bay the sense of emptiness and yearning that mark this centre.

The belly centre (sometimes called the gut or body centre) is the focus of our instinctual intelligence, or sense of being, as contrasted with thinking and feeling. We experience ourselves physically in relation to people and the environment through this centre. It is the source of our energy and power to act in the physical world.

Belly-based types (8, 9, 1), whose focus is on being, tend to 'be' in the world through action. Their instinct is to do, and they may speak of basing decisions and actions on a gut feeling even when they have thought them through in detail. They are known as 'self-forgetting' types as they may be unaware of their own truest priorities. Being active in the world is fuelled by and mitigates the anger which, at least for Type Ones and Type Nines, only occasionally surfaces in direct expression.

How the Enneagram works:
Each type's structure

Head, heart and belly in each person

Much could be said about how personality develops, and the Enneagram can be elegantly and accurately related to current psychological and developmental theory, including neurobiology as a potential source of innate developmental imperatives. However, this book is concerned with the crucial, and fundamental, insight that underlying any developmental factors (nurture) there is a clear, innate framework or structure (nature), and this is defined by the centres of cognition and perception in the head, heart and belly of each of us.

Although each type favours one centre, everybody contains and is affected by the head, heart and belly centres in themselves. The Enneagram describes the different qualities of the centres in each human being – a 'structure' common to us all – and then shows how this manifests differently in the different types.

Effectively, there are 'two of us' inside us all: the essential self, known as soul, or inner witness; and the personality which believes itself to be 'who I am', but is in fact changeable and clearly acquired.

Of these two selves, the personality manifests through habitual narrow ways of thinking, feeling (emotions) and surviving (gut reactions). These are called respectively Fixation, Passion and Instinctual subtypes, and are the source of the repeating patterns in our lives.

Describing our essential selves, the head and heart centres both have a 'holy opposite', a particular aspect of Essence lost sight of as personality developed. These are known as Holy Idea and Holy Virtue (or simply Virtue). The 'spiritual' belly does not have a particular name, nor nine different qualities, as it simply taps into and provides us with the life force, which is the same for all people.

Actually, the Holy Idea and Virtue are more like a 'holy seed' than 'holy opposite', as they were with us at birth and name the essential or divine qualities of our true self. We simply forgot this as we learnt to cope with the world and developed our personality defence structure. The personality protects and masks the essential self but also mimics it, like a mirror reflecting back to front, by looking for the forgotten aspects in the outside world instead of within. This is the basis of the differences between the nine types.

To summarise: one underlying structure for all types, with nine very distinct and different ways of manifesting it; and for each of the nine, an essential self with spiritual qualities, and a psychological self whose narrow focus of attention is unconsciously trying to mimic these innate forgotten qualities.

The diagrams below summarise the key symbolic words assigned to these various aspects of type, which are explained in detail in the relevant chapters.

The head centre: Fixation and Holy Idea

The Fixation indicates the tenor of the personality's habitual mental preoccupation or focus of attention. It could be described as the hamster in the mental hamster wheel. The Holy Idea represents the state of awareness that is experienced, rather than thought of, by the spiritual head centre when it is free of the Fixation.

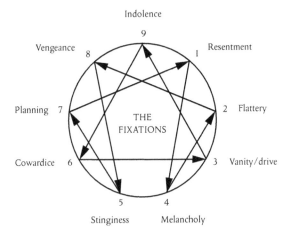

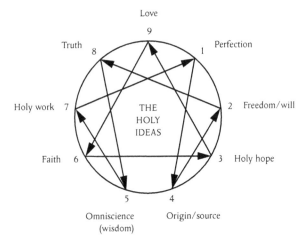

The heart centre: Passion and Holy Virtue

The habitual underlying emotion of the heart centre is called its Passion. Early Christians were well aware of this aspect, being the nine interruptions to the life of prayer mentioned by Evagrius Ponticus. They now correspond to the seven capital tendencies or 'deadly sins', plus fear and deceit, also known as vainglory. The essential state of being experienced in the heart is called the Holy Virtue or Virtue of Essence.

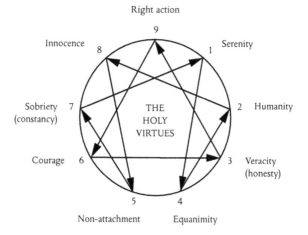

The belly centre: Subtypes

The word 'subtypes' refers to three survival instincts connected to the belly centre of each Enneagram type (giving us 27 subtypes).

Survival – the matter of life and death – is taken care of in the last resort by instinctive, unconscious gut reaction. The nine Fixations (head centre) and Passions (heart centre) define the overall personality concerns, and can be relatively easily recognised as 'what I do'. The subtypes define three often very different ways of manifesting each type, and because the behaviours arising from them are indeed a matter of life and death (or so it seems to the unconscious mind), they often seem like 'that's who I am', carry a great deal of energy with them and can be harder to recognise in oneself.

These basic instincts concern survival in three fundamental arenas:

1. Self-preservation, 'the right to exist':

    - physical survival

    - energy focuses on material well-being, nurture, home.

2. Social, 'the right to belong':

    - since humans are tribal animals, survival also depends on acceptance in the tribe

    - energy focuses on the social group and social causes.

3. Sexual, 'the right to be loved':

    - the instinct to survive through what is newly created through one-to-one relationships, whether that's a baby, an idea or simply validation by another

    - energy focuses on intensity of connection with the other.

Each of us tends to focus on one of these in particular, depending on where we perceived or experienced the greatest threat to, or denial of, our essential self as we grew up. Were we fed, kept warm, nurtured well; were we accepted by the family as who we were; were our attempts to attract unconditional love and friendship accepted?

Currently, there is some debate as to whether the subtype focus is innately present at birth, whether it is developmental and a result of our environment, or a combination of the two, just as our individual adult persona is. Whichever the case, the result is that whilst all three arenas are important for happy functioning in life, *one* of them will unconsciously be seen as the greatest possible source of pain or threat. Therefore, it draws a lot of our attention and energy to it, and seems also to be the greatest source of our happiness and satisfaction.

They also provide ways of channelling the energy of the Passion – which in its raw form would be too hard to bear. Thus they alleviate the pain and (seem to) make logical the biased focus of attention of the personality. With all the force of instinctive survival behind them, when they are working we feel secure, energised and 'real'. The raw energy of the Passion drives the subtype behaviours, which in turn dissipate the energy and obscure the pain of the Passion from everyday consciousness – since they seem such a natural and authentic expression of 'who I am'.

This being the case, subtype behaviour is the most unconscious and automatic, seems most 'true to ourselves' (who I am, rather than what I do) and forms the greatest barrier to our reconnection with Essence and our own soul. Because of this, and because the belly centre, once freed from the limitations and concerns of personality, provides the energy for transformation, the understanding of subtypes is vital in our search for the return to Essence.

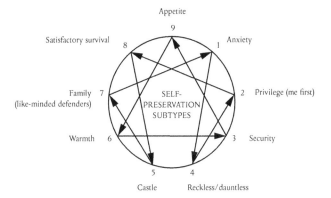

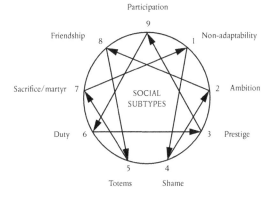

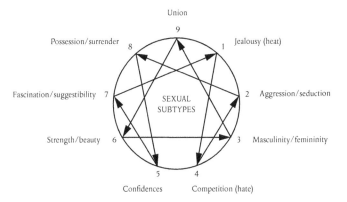

How the Enneagram works:
Psychological and spiritual growth

The Enneagram is an instrument of great subtlety, yet the central premise it is based on is very simple: that our personality was developed to protect our higher self and is inseparably linked to it.

There is also one simple observation that allows us to use this knowledge, and it is not unique to the Enneagram. This is that we are two 'people' inside. One is the personality, which identifies itself with our thoughts, feelings and sensations; the other is the inner witness, sometimes called the observer, Essence or soul. This is not the part of our personality which watches and comments on our lives, but an awareness that is neither thought, feeling nor sensation, yet *is* us in a way the personality is not.

This difference between our psychological and spiritual natures is only apparent. Both are integral to who we are. While we are alive, we need a personality, to mediate between our higher self and the world and help us get things done, but we also need to recognise its nature. It is a set of tools, some of which work very well to help us through life, and some of which don't. Though we adopted them to help us keep safe, by the time we are adult they've become a hindrance, not a help. The psychological task is to recognise which aspects do not serve us, and let them go.

To transform something, first you have to know what is so. If you wish to make a journey, it helps to have a map of the terrain, to know where 'here' is on the map (and 'there', if you want to get there) and what obstacles you may encounter.

This is a major part of the Enneagram's value: it is a map of your particular terrain. In the same way that traversing the Sahara doesn't require wet-weather gear, so, if your particular habit of mind is one of fear, it will not help much to work on your anger, and vice versa. Envy is only a major issue for some people, pride for others, and so on.

In relation to Essence, our 'higher self', all mystical traditions describe the threefold attributes of the soul (or 'true' self for those who doubt the existence of a soul). The Enneagram uses the Christian terminology; I include the next best-known triad of words – sat, chit, ananda: being, consciousness, bliss – in the illustration below, but could have drawn on any tradition.

The spiritual gifts – the Essence of each of the nine types – are variations on these three themes. In truth, when we achieve Presence, arrive at Now (which has been the primary spiritual focus for as long as spiritual writings have existed, so presumably also long before that), we find all three centres united and all three gifts available. Still, we need a way home to that place, and the nine Holy Ideas and Virtues offer the best gateway home, with each of the centres having a particular theme and related spiritual practices.

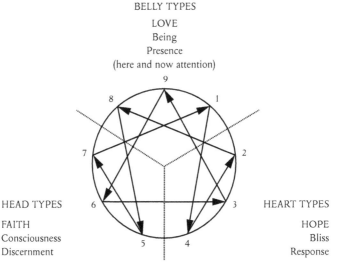

BELLY TYPES
LOVE
Being
Presence
(here and now attention)

HEAD TYPES
FAITH
Consciousness
Discernment

HEART TYPES
HOPE
Bliss
Response

The head centre corresponds spiritually to the 'third eye' or visualisation centre used in, for example, Tibetan Buddhist meditations and many of the practices of Ignatian spirituality. The head centre knows what is real and trusts it absolutely. Creation is trustworthy. This is the meaning of faith. Faith 'knows' and requires no proof, because faith knows only what is true – what *is* – and discerns the significance of what is in this unique moment. This wordless discernment lets us know how the world works and thus the wisdom to act courageously in harmony with what the world needs.

The heart centre is the spiritual heart centre opened in Sufi and many Christian practices. The liturgy, chanting, devotional prayer and adoration all access the spiritual heart. We in the West associate the heart with love; in the Enneagram, Love – unconditional love – belongs to the belly. It's a *given*. It's where we come from, who we are, where we return to. So what is the true name for the movement/bliss of the heart? The yearning called 'love' is actually the outward movement of the soul in its urge to reunite, and heart types know that it's all about relationship, the unfolding in space and time as a result of our interweaving. The heart wishes to reach out, respond, and create anew in hope.

The belly centre has been almost forgotten in the West as an organ of spiritual perception. It corresponds to the area known as, for example, *hara* in Japan and *dan tian* in China, and is the focus of Zen practices. In Christianity this centre is not named except in the phrase 'bowels of compassion', but breath meditation (breathing the One Breath) accesses it, as do centring prayer and contemplative prayer. Love knows I exist, as a necessary and connected, inalienable part of the whole of creation. I am that I am. The gifts of the belly centre are all to do with the actual nature of reality, of existence, of Being, of Presence, of Now.

Gurdjieff said that if we can identify our chief feature, much of the work has already been accomplished, and the Enneagram provides the key to this. The inner observer differentiates between personality (built of memories, ideas, plans, dreams) and Essence, and this is the key to spiritual growth. Thus, through self-observation, we can recognise the personality's automatic reactions and use them as reminders of our essential qualities. In this way we regain the ability to respond to life from an unbiased perspective in tune with our true selves.

If we are skilful, the inner observer can help us to release patterns and bring out hidden and unused potentials. Knowing the terrain makes our efforts much easier and more accurate. It is not a question of transcending or subduing the personality, but of befriending it and learning which way it points us.

Finally, whether we approach the work of personal growth as primarily psychological, spiritual or both, the 'proof of the pudding' is in the personal world. We can understand our background influences or meditate for hours daily. Unless it increases our humane-ness and loving kindness, unless our daily actions, thoughts and relationships are more harmonious and lovingly creative, it is not growth.

Chapter 2

Type One
The Perfectionist

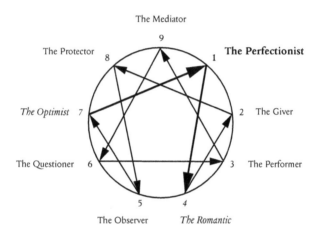

Outward appearance

Type Ones are responsible, strong-minded, hard-working people who have high internal standards. They take life seriously and can appear irritable, intense, judgemental, controlled, self-righteous and compulsive in their striving for perfection.

Sensitive to criticism, they judge themselves harshly and find it hard to accept compliments or to acknowledge their own accomplishments. Wanting to get things right and be liked, they can seem curiously melancholy under their surface sharpness.

Ones do not mark time. Their acute awareness of imperfections motivates them to improve things, and they will take responsibility for doing so even when it seems a never-ending thankless task. Even their leisure, which is infrequent, is often used for self-improvement. They take pleasure in a job well done.

> *'The doing itself is exciting, it's creative. Our team's integrity is high, we're known because we do the best. There's a lot of planning and thinking it through first to get it just right – and that's the real fun. Doing it according to plan is also rewarding. Detail is important – it's the doing not the goal that's important.'*

Integrity and authenticity are important to Ones. The world is viewed in terms of right and wrong, with no middle ground, and they can be zealous in supporting a cause if their sense of justice is violated. They seem to feel that if they work hard enough they can put anything right, and that they are the only ones who will bother.

Self-criticism is a constant feature in their lives, and they expect other people's feedback, however mild, to contain criticism – though if overtly criticised they become angry, as no one knows their faults and mistakes more clearly than themselves. Their criticality of others may well be judgemental, but it may also disguise a desire to help perfect something in someone they care about, which they know is already good.

Despite their energetic activity, Ones often procrastinate or get caught up in details for fear of getting something wrong. Their standards cover every aspect of life and are personal and different for each One. However, their rules are 'the' rules, and believing that 'everyone knows' the rules, they resent people who get away with breaking them.

> *'If people criticise or doubt me, either I work on that to get better or my anger comes out and I think, "You just don't see it."'*

Ones are often critical of authority. They want high ethics and clear guidelines so they can measure themselves against the correct standard. Given a clear brief, they become angry if it is altered, although *'if there's good reason for a change and it's logical, we* can *be flexible – especially if flexibility's one of the given parameters'*.

They usually seem controlled, not only in their actions and environment but emotionally, and can become confused when things are out of control. Having put so much energy into making things go right, they want to blame others when anything goes wrong, but blame is inconsistent with taking responsibility. Moreover, when things do go wrong, they feel it must be their fault even when they know it's not.

> *'I keep internal control of emotions… My concern is if my feelings should get out they will affect the situation, or other people's reactions will affect the situation, and I need to have control over it – events must be what I think they should be. Control is about getting things going the way they're supposed to be going. But I'm not interested in controlling other people. And my emotions…if they do get out, they might never stop.'*

Ones do not seem to have much pleasure in their lives, but there is satisfaction in, for example, helping people with problems, or study, and the occasional perfect moment.

> *'I enjoy knowing things, especially high or hard things; fine art, music; those six seconds when the team rowed as one man; simple things like nature; small perfect things – one flower given to me.'*

Unaware Ones can be cynical, punitive, self-righteous, cold, bigoted, controlling, anxious or angry, obsessive-compulsive, sarcastic and dogmatic. An example would be the fundamentalist religious zealot.

Aware Ones can be inspiring, caring, wise and ethical, self-disciplined, productive, discriminating and serene. They are able to celebrate and encourage excellence everywhere, from a warm and beautiful home to mankind's highest endeavours.

Inner concerns and childhood scenarios

Ones became aware in infancy that they were not considered perfect, and their attention focused on imperfection and becoming worthy of love. They report having felt themselves continually under a critical gaze, never acknowledged for doing anything good but told to do better. They may have had overtly angry or critical parents, or have interpreted lack of love as disapproval. Sometimes they were the oldest child, expected to take responsibility – and the blame – for all their siblings.

Even when their family background was loving and supportive, they became preoccupied with trying to be what was considered 'good'. Young Ones internalised a critical gaze and monitored themselves in an attempt to pre-empt criticism, by doing nothing that could be considered wrong.

> *'To be perfect would have been the only way I could have ended the constant criticality of my parents. They always wanted me to achieve something, and it was never enough – they said "Fine" and went to the next thing – there was no glory in having done it. It was like a constant treadmill. Love was never mentioned – just to be accepted would have seemed enough.'*

Emotions became dangerous. They learned to see them as bad, and even pleasant emotions could trigger impulsive and incorrect action, and were therefore dangerous. The more emotions were suppressed, the worse they seemed, and therefore the more reason there was to suppress them.

As Ones continued to 'fail', their set of rules expanded. Self-forgetting consisted of replacing intuitive truth and real priorities with adopted correct behaviour and focusing on what was wrong in themselves, their actions and the outside world.

Passion and Fixation: Anger and resentment

Ones are belly types who suppress their 'gut' reactions and emotions in favour of rationality, and often think of themselves as head types at first.

Anger, which in its cleanest form is a freeing cathartic energy that can fuel growth, is the foremost emotion for belly types and is also the emotional preoccupation of Ones. Yet they report that they are rarely, if ever, angry, even when others can feel it. Their initial anger at being unrecognised was suppressed and displaced into anger at themselves, through which it validates self-forgetting and the censoring of all emotions. Occasionally, real anger will erupt, usually after months or years of suppression. This can be frightening as it has all the force of its accumulation and is often misdirected.

> 'Others will feel it's directed at them, but it may have started months ago and just coming to a head now, and I really can't tell where it started or what it's really about.'

Some Perfectionists give themselves permission to feel and express 'justified' anger, where they occupy the moral high ground and it is others who are imperfect. Other feelings are also suppressed, though some Ones have a 'trapdoor' between the emotions and the judging mind. From time to time they take a break somewhere they will not be seen by people who could later judge them, and just enjoy themselves. For a few, the grip of the inner critic is so strong that they have amnesia of these periods of release.

Resentment is rationalised anger, and more easily recognised by the One. Unacceptable rage is transmuted into acceptable thoughts, from frustration and hatred of hypocrisy to irritability and resentment. These, together with the righteous wrath that they sometimes express, can be justified because they are 'caused by' external circumstances.

Living in the head feels safe to Ones and enables constant comparison with the rules, which are held in the mind. Ones continually compare themselves with others as well as their internal standards. *'With anyone, I know whether I am better or worse than they. Both make me angry.'* The habit of resentment allows them to project the sensations of anger on to the outside world.

> *'When I was young I got into a lot of trouble by being extremely intolerant in my view of the world. Not only did people do things the wrong way – I didn't tolerate fools gladly – but they seemed to do it on purpose. I thought half the people I knew should be locked up or sacked. It's only in later years I've realised my way isn't the only way, and that maybe a lot of the trouble was caused by me.'*

Some Ones express their resentment in open criticism and irritation; others will pointedly and carefully follow the rules to demonstrate how things *should* be done.

Stress

> *'No matter what I do, I just can't get this [situation or thing] right.'*

Under stress, Ones take on the emotional idealism of Type Four, the Romantic, emphasising their belief that perfection is unattainable and that somehow they are unworthy. Their focus shifts to relationship or emotions and their feeling of being unlovable. They can become depressed, feeling that they are worthless and will never get it right, so life is pointless.

> 'If I just knew what the right way was, then surely she would love me… If I'm flawed, then no one would love me; how could they love me if I'm not perfect? But without her love I won't be able to do anything worthwhile, so it's impossible. I just can't see any meaning in anything any more. All I can remember are the things I didn't do perfectly… It seems so hopeless.'

On the positive side, taking on Four's qualities can enhance Ones' appreciation of and longing for perfection, and opens up their feelings. They say even the darkest feelings can be a relief and a source of aesthetic enjoyment.

Security

Some Ones barely recognise Type Seven, the Optimist, in their make-up, even when in an emotionally secure relationship. Others delight in the respite it gives from the critic, and seek out Sevens as friends. When they do allow themselves to relax into emotional security, they can have fun for a while. Pleasurable activities for Ones are things like sport, being in nature and alone, breaking the rules, intellectual pursuits and imagining future options.

> 'Freedom from the critic feels wonderful – it doesn't often happen at home, because there's the family to worry about – but going on holiday with the family, somehow I can drop the rules and just have fun. The children always say how different I am. And I love to use my intellect to help others by considering all the options…and to imagine things to share with my partner. It's not necessary to actually do them.'

Subtypes

The Passion of anger is primarily about feeling the world, and oneself, to be imperfect, when there is an underlying unconscious feeling that I/it 'could' be perfect, or at least perfectible. Anger is essentially the human reaction to boundaries being transgressed, and a person who knows what is 'right' lives with boundaries constantly transgressed by themselves and others. Anger turns the unconscious 'could' into a conscious, permanent, driven and unattainable 'should'.

Dissipating the raw energy and obscuring anger from everyday consciousness, the subtype allows Ones not to have to face the actual experience of the 'imperfect' feeling of rage at loss of perfection.

Self-preservation: Anxiety/worry

The energy of anger is diverted into anxiety about personal security: getting things right, having exactly what one needs, keeping the job, looking after the family and so on. It may look like fear but is more of a permanent resentful worrying.

> 'I so much need to be sure I'll have everything I could possibly need available when I go away that packing becomes an ordeal. It takes weeks, and I hate it. If I don't have something I need, I worry continually and will do anything to get it – it feels as though my survival is at stake until I have it.'

Social: Non-adaptability

Wanting to ally themselves with the worthy group and support the politically, socially or spiritually correct cause, social Ones can experience confusion, frustration or outright (justifiable) anger aimed at the group and/or at themselves. They criticise the group for not being perfect, and themselves for not being able to adapt themselves to the group customs.

> *'I think I'm extremely adaptable – I take pride in it – but I have a lot of anger about my disappointment that the group I'd chosen didn't live up to its own standards. I want to join in and also to stand apart and criticise in an attempt to improve it. Usually, I would leave, but not before I'd fought the leadership to try and get the group back on line – the ideal line.'*

Sexual: Jealousy/heat

Sexual subtype Ones, idealising the perfect connection to the one person (friend or spouse), fear that other people will be seen as more attractive, intelligent and desirable than themselves. Anger is channelled into a jealous scanning to make sure they are still wanted, and any imagined rejection produces an unthinking 'heat' of anger – though it is rarely recognised as anger, or even jealousy, since both are 'wrong' emotions.

> *'At a gathering, if a good friend passes me by for someone else, I become angry at them, resentful of the person they are talking to, and if they're not with anyone else, the image of someone who is more attractive and intelligent than me goes through my head and I'm angry at that imaginary person. With my wife, I don't say anything, but this kind of resentment builds up and I'm comparing myself to any man I see her talking to.'*

Relationships

Though Ones desire relationships, they find it hard to trust the world because it often seems people do not mean what they say. They also feel they may be unworthy of friendship because they themselves are not perfect.

> *'If I were to be able to say, "The hell with what anyone thinks of me," it would be so much easier to join the group.'*

They tend to back off after initial closeness to see if the other person considers them worthy of friendship, and if the person is also worthy. Both are proven if the other person contacts them. This, together with their often aloof or sarcastic presentation, may result in the pain of losing people who were potentially close friends.

Ones need to be met energetically by friends, since it shows the other person is equally involved. It also means a great deal to Ones to be told they are valued as they are and their company enjoyed for its own sake. Trusted friends can help them express the deep emotions, which they fear to show in case it drives others away, not realising they often tacitly broadcast anger and a confused hurt.

They may also be unaware that it can be difficult to relate to their critical nit-picking side. Often Ones, caring deeply that friends should fulfil their highest potential, offer constructive criticism with a loving intention that is easily misread. If this is understood, they can flourish in a co-mentor friendship where each learns from and contributes to the other.

Perfectionism in intimate relationships can cause problems and misunderstandings unless the ground rules are well established. Ones long for the perfect relationship, and when flaws appear, as they inevitably will, they look to see if they are doing anything wrong. If not, it is easy for them to resent and blame their partner.

> 'There's a need to be in control so I can make sure it comes out perfectly. We found it's important to have clear ground rules – even if they are uncertain and that's part of the rules. Who does what, is responsible for what, must be defined – otherwise, I'll take on responsibility so that it goes perfectly. I can leave it if it's agreed it's not my responsibility.'

Another potential barrier to intimacy exists for those who learned, and internalised, that sexuality is bad. As Ones become intimate, this is one of the many rules they may have to question to create a loving and equal relationship where they can support their partner's highest potential while accepting that they too are lovable.

Things Ones can do to help themselves grow

- Find a friend or therapist who can help you depersonalise issues for which you are blaming yourself or others.

- Join a group that encourages expression of immediate emotions, including anger, in a safe environment.

- Notice your thinking in terms of either/or, right/ wrong, and include more sides to the story.

- Start to appreciate that differences are not necessarily errors or faults.

- Notice that resentment at others who break the rules may mask a wish to do what they are doing.

- Notice yourself going silent and controlled, and use it as a signal to find out what you are angry about.

- If you feel angry or irritated, see if there is something you're not allowing yourself, or if it is displaced from a large to a smaller issue.

- Take time to observe the critical mind in action, and disidentify with it – use its precision to remind yourself of your achievements and skills instead.

- Learn to allow yourself minor errors without blame.

- Schedule time out from compulsive activity, to be able to think about your own real priorities.

- Put play and pleasure in your list of oughts, until you can allow them for their own sakes.

- Ask people how you're coming across: if you are surprised, consider whether it reflects a feeling you are stifling.

- Explore how you are as a person rather than in relation to your rules and activities: what do I like, want, need, feel, *really* think about this?

- Question your rules, and remind yourself that what is 'right' is not necessarily what is desirable or appropriate.

Things friends can do to support Ones

- Support them in all of the above.

- Admit to your own criticisms and mistakes.

- Provide them with a non-judgemental space.

- Point out what is positive, both around them and in themselves.

- Let them know they are likable, even though not perfect.

- Remind them the goal of growth is to be whole, not perfect.

- Invite them out to have fun, whatever that may be for them.

Holy Virtue and Holy Idea:
Serenity and perfection

Serenity is not the cessation of emotion but a state of awareness that allows all feelings to come and go in the body and heart, and be fully experienced as they do, without judging some as good or pleasant and others as bad or unpleasant. Ones who learn to release their anger, once the backlog of suppressed feeling has been cleared, experience a sense of being fully energised and yet light of heart and body, a joyful acceptance of all facets of being and an ability to engage with life and feelings fully and serenely.

When fully engaged with life, Ones realise that everything, including themselves, is already perfect even in its imperfection. The habit of resentment can be hard to let go of. If the mind is not the correct source of criteria for perfection, and if it may not assign blame, how can perfection be attained? When Ones allow themselves to accept that the mind, which is partial and imperfect, cannot produce perfection, they experience and celebrate the **perfection** in themselves and everything around them.

Perfection perceives the fact and the lovingness of reality, sees the essential rightness of what is and what unfolds, and accepts and trusts what is. The **serene** heart is calm, at one with itself and creation, secure in the rightness of reality and its own ability to express itself truly and harmoniously.

Chapter 3

Type Two
The Giver

The Mediator

The Protector 8 — 9 — 1 The Perfectionist

The Optimist 7 — 2 **The Giver**

The Questioner 6 — 3 The Performer

5 — 4

The Observer — *The Romantic*

Outward appearance

Type Twos usually appear outgoing, cheerful, energetic, friendly, confident, entertaining and, above all, helpful. They freely offer their time and energy as well as material things, and gifts are always carefully chosen to suit the recipient's tastes. Twos prefer giving to receiving, and seem to have no needs of their own: they are independent and capable, and are happiest when meeting others' needs.

> *'Even if I am alone, which is not often, I'm thinking of other people and how what I'm doing links me to them. Say I'm gardening – I'll be thinking about the cuttings I'm going to give to the woman next door...'*

Although they appear self-sufficient, their world is focused around relationships. They actively seek approval, and their skills and successes are usually in the service of another person. Twos have a genuine empathic awareness of others' needs and feelings, and tune themselves to meet those needs. They do this not only in material ways but even more fundamentally by being the kind of person the other would like to know. They are different with different people, though not with any sense of deception.

> *'I'm not lying – what I show people really is a part of me, it's just not all of me. It's great: I have lots of different sorts of friends who wouldn't get on together at all. The down side is if there are two different people I like in the same place, it can get very confusing.'*

Most Twos would not consider themselves proud, but combining no (apparent) needs themselves with certainty that they can meet everyone else's, they can seem slightly superior. They may become aloof if a relationship gets too intimate, saying they need their freedom, but actually being unwilling to risk rejection by revealing more of themselves. In addition, Twos are selective about who they connect with, and will often choose special, challenging or unattainable people.

They can go to extraordinary lengths to help, or to attract, another person, and find it almost impossible to refuse if someone asks for something. They can exhaust themselves by taking on too much, and may feel taken for granted if they keep giving to someone who does not seem to notice, or who backs away from so much generosity. When either of these happens, Twos can express a degree of emotionality or anger that surprises other people.

Usually, it feels good to be the focus of a Two's attention: not only do they meet people's real needs (often before a person even knows they have that need), but they see and support the highest potential in their friends. However, from other types' point of view, it seems unbelievable the Two is really focused on someone else to that extent, and it can feel manipulative. They want contact and response, and can be intrusive trying to find out what another wants.

Unaware Twos can be hysterical, manipulative, smothering or ambitious give-to-get personalities. The archetype is the self-sacrificing intrusive mother, who complains that her family never appreciates her help or gives anything back.

Aware Twos are loving and empathic, truly supportive and appropriate in their giving. They are perceptive, adaptable, loyal and selfless helpers, whether as friends, bosses or the power behind the throne.

Inner concerns and childhood scenarios

Twos have learned that to be loved they must meet the needs of others, and so have discounted their personal needs, and in a sense themselves, in favour of giving what will gain approval. They may have had a needy parent, demanding to be looked after; or they may have needed to disarm a domineering or critical figure; or their parent(s) may have been distant, absorbed in other things.

As heart types, Twos are naturally sensitive to others' feelings. In early childhood they learned to become acutely aware of the emotional and physical cues of important adults, and respond to those cues by presenting a persona that would gain the adult's attention and approval.

> *'When there are too many needs for one person to meet, still I have to meet all those needs to avoid a certain look – they don't like me. If you don't like what I do, you don't like me. They are inseparable.'*

Passion and Fixation: Pride and flattery

Pride for Twos is the inner certainty that, because of their deep sensitivity and ability to tune in accurately to others, they can fulfil other people's needs better than anyone else. This is coupled with the belief that they have very few, if any, needs of their own. They believe they are independent whilst others depend on them, and find it hard to realise that in fact they are dependent on others, not only for approval but also for their sense of who they are from moment to moment.

> *'I only get a sense of self by other people's gaze on me. When I get attention, I can start to define who I am. How I feel about myself depends on the reaction I get.'*

Pride is also a motivating force for Twos to do everything extremely well. It is not a moral imperative, but because *'it's better that way, that's how it should be done in the pattern of things'*. They need to excel in public so they are approved and accepted.

> *'It filters down into everything I do. It's very important for me to do things well. It could be my work, or my family, home improvement, playing with the children – whatever. Habitually, it's always been about what I got back for that. What I'm trying to do now is do it for its own sake. It's difficult.'*

Giving for its own sake, rather than for what they receive in return, means Twos have to admit to themselves that they have needs, and then learn to articulate what they are, both day to day and in the long term. This can be puzzling and humiliating for someone whose habit is to put all their attention on other people whilst asserting their own independence.

'I tried to look inside for what I felt, and it was terrifying. There was just nothing – there didn't seem to be anybody there at all, just a big empty hole. So much for my inner resources.'

When Twos' unconscious needs are not being met, or they begin to acknowledge them, hysteria starts to rise. This can range from confusion to overblown emotionality.

'...but it's surface, there's nothing real about it, there's dissociation physically, I'm not in my body, I'm distant, not really listening, spaced out – I'm nowhere. It looks very intense and dramatic, but this is not the same as when I'm really in touch with my own deep feelings.'

Pride underlies Twos' selectivity in giving, and is supported by a vivid emotional imagination whereby they idealise people they want to know.

'Challenge is a big factor. Idealisation as well – putting a glamour over the selected person and making up who you want them to be. Both things let me feel I've been wonderful enough to get them.'

Flattery as a habit of mind may or may not be a conscious flattering of others. It relates to Twos' ability to make others feel good by appealing to their inner preferences and recognising and supporting their highest potential.

Twos are quick to praise, either overtly or implicitly, through seeking others out and meeting their needs. They see others' abilities, but have difficulty acknowledging and developing their own abilities for themselves.

'I would never have got my PhD if she hadn't told me to, that it would add credibility to the company as a whole. I had been

> *wanting to do it for some time, and it was actually easy, but there hadn't seemed any point when it was just for me.'*

There is a seductive flavour to Twos' charm. They 'know' they can make anyone feel good around them, and being focused on avoiding rejection, they are skilled at disarming people.

> *'I rarely meet anyone I don't like – I reframe the ones I don't into a way that I can forgive them. I can manipulate even my own thoughts. And I can manipulate your arguments easily to avert your anger from me.'*

Twos can meet the needs even of people who don't seem to have any, by being the kind of person they like to know and making them feel good about themselves:

> *'I appeal to their intellect, or their emotional life, or be fun for them to be with – I find something which will appeal to them.'*

Stress

> *'No matter what I do, this person doesn't give me the approval signals that I'm (unconsciously) looking for.'*

While hysteria is a sign of stress rising in Twos, it is still part of the central type. When real stress hits, they take on characteristics of Eight, the Protector, and can become domineering, irritable and finally angry. This does not fit well with their normal charming persona, and some Twos find anger in themselves or others very frightening, avoiding it almost at all costs. Others find it easier to express.

> *'Anger builds up and up and up in me, and when it explodes, it's terrifying, it's mortifying. It's also often misplaced – it's directed at the cat or the other driver, not the person it should be. But it can build up over the littlest thing. I blow off a lot of my anger in traffic, for example.'*

Under stress, too, the Eight-ish desire not to be controlled magnifies Twos' desire for freedom, and they will fight for their own position and resist other people's demands in a way they normally would not.

Security

Twos move towards Four, the Romantic, in emotional security. For some, the increased emotionality, especially the romantic yearning of the Four personality, is very painful.

> '*I just melt emotionally and want to cry all the time. It can feel debilitating, and I almost want to push it away so I can feel together again.*'

Others find a release into the artistic side of themselves very energising:

> '*...out come the water-colours, and I'm gone for hours...or I'll plan the complete redecoration of the house, or a meal that would make the Roux brothers sit up and beg... It feels very creative.*'

Ironically, the Four's push–pull way of relating may emphasise Twos' tendency to pull back from intimacy, even in emotional security, while their yearning for true connection is deeper than ever.

Subtypes

The Passion of pride is primarily about maintaining the feeling that '*"Who I am" is more skilled at meeting another's needs than anyone else – they couldn't get along without me – therefore I'm worthy of love.*'

Dissipating the raw energy and obscuring pride from everyday consciousness, the subtype allows Twos not to have to face the actual experience of feeling unlovable because they don't and can't meet everyone's needs; and that they themselves have needs and might be unlovable if they're needy.

Self-preservation: Privilege / me first

Twos express pride in the area of basic survival by making sure they are at the head of the queue, not sharing certain personal things, and securing the survival of pride itself by not asking for help until survival is definitely threatened. Insecurity about meeting one's own needs is suppressed in favour of meeting the needs of others who can ensure survival.

> 'If I waited and didn't take care of it, there wouldn't be enough for me. But I won't ask my family for help – I'd feel guilty, and a failure. The few times I've blown up at my wife because she just was asking for too much, I've always felt a bit ashamed afterwards.'

Social: Ambition

Social Twos seek out and attach themselves to important people in the group. Ambition is expressed through being the power behind the throne and meeting the needs of the most prestigious people present. It may also take the form of belonging to groups with status and taking pride in social position.

> 'I decided early on that I was going to marry a high society Anglican priest. I wouldn't even go out with someone who wasn't applying for, or at [the best] College. I now see it was so that I would be important to all those "special" people.'

Sexual: Aggression / seduction

Twos who focus on one-to-one relationships take pride in being able to make anyone want to be friends or lovers with them. It's a very selective and seductive approach, and aggressive in that once Twos have chosen a person, they will keep going until that person is 'caught'.

> *'I can make any man feel he's a king, if only for a night. I can get him just by holding my glass a certain way; and he won't forget me. For longer-term relationships, I do a lot of research into what they like. It's addictive. Once a relationship is over, it's "just one more time…" There's a lot of energy involved, and if I stop, what would I do with it? There's panic at the thought…'*

Relationships

The approval and well-being of colleagues, friends and intimates is paramount for Twos. At work, for example, they work hard to be liked by supporting the right people and doing well themselves while promoting the welfare of those around them. If a boss 'needs' them to be successful, they are.

Friendship and relationships are the heart of Twos' lives, but in the long term putting other people's needs first has a variety of negative effects. Beneath the generally happy and confident public face, Twos suffer painful emotions and personal dilemmas.

> *'People's expectations can push me into sadness, and anger. They get used to what I give and take it for granted, and in the end there's no appreciation. I'm not understood. And if I get angry, they might leave.'*

Twos experience anxiety about getting things right in the relationship, particularly when it seems that overtures might not be working. Moreover, their tendency to think about the relationship when the other person is not present means they can create a fantasy relationship and be confused and worried when the reality is brought home to them.

> *'My thoughts can spiral right out. Sometimes I'm so far out I can't get back into myself. It really helps to have someone bring me back here – but I need to be alone to know what I need.'*

Out of touch with their own needs and wants, believing they have none, Twos unconsciously seek out people who, by virtue of who they are, will fulfil their needs.

> *'...and here's an aspect of myself that I need, don't express, but I want it, and by bringing out that part of my personality to meet your need...'*

Friends of Twos often feel there is a debt, an imbalance of generosity, as though whenever they give the Two something, the Two just has to top it slightly. Since Twos have difficulty receiving (they don't have needs and wonder what might be wanted from them in return) and don't recognise the compulsiveness of their giving, it can be hard to equalise the situation.

Givers can find it hard to relax into intimate relationships and are often attracted to unattainable partners – someone who travels a lot, or a triangle, where they don't have to be 'on' for that person all the time. They live so much with their attention on others that, *'When intimacy comes, what do I really feel? Who knows...?'* Even sexual intimacy can be experienced as part of the giving-to-get. *'Even though I like sex, I never knew till meeting Jim in my forties what the term "making love" meant. I'd always just "had sex".'*

As intimacy becomes established, Twos have to confront the pain of discovering what they want and asking for it.

> *'Leaving the house at different times hurts more than leaving at your time rather than mine. Or going to see a film – it's easier not to go, even when I do want to, than to go anyway on my own.'*

They also have to face the reality of who their partner is.

> *'Before we met, he was a Greek god, but I never let on: passionate, powerful. But when this image falls apart, then what do I really feel? Is this really love? I created a challenge for me to live up to that didn't exist. He felt daunted trying to live up to it, and it took several years of marriage before I was willing to see him as he is. It's been a relief to learn to be ourselves – and hard work but worthwhile to discover love doesn't depend on being a certain way.'*

Things Twos can do to help themselves grow

- Develop interests and activities that are meaningful to you on your own, and do them on your own.

- Make time to be alone and bring your attention back inside – for example, meditating; notice the anxiety and desire to focus out again.

- Notice your own achievements and their worth.

- Enumerate and value your own skills.

- Consciously do things well for their own and your own sake alone.

- Notice your hysteria when it rises, and use it as a cue to ask, 'What do I need right now?'

- Notice flattery and the tendency to be helpless or second to others, and that dependency is manipulation.

- Look beneath your initial emotional reactions, particularly anger, which may be masking real feelings.

- Tell people what you need and allow them to give it to you: learn to enjoy receiving.

- Notice when 'multiple personalities' conflict, and develop a consistent presentation, true to yourself and not changing to please.

- Remember that real love isn't dependent on you being a certain way.

Things friends can do to support Twos

- Encourage them in all of the above.

- Mirror them back to themselves: 'This is what I see in you, it's constant, it doesn't change, it's good, you can exercise this.'

- Remind them of their capabilities and give approval – mean it, and keep doing it.

- Let them know you like them for themselves, the whole person.

- Don't ask what they need – just do something for them.

- When they are in hysteria or spaced out, provide a focusing device by asking questions.

- When they are down on themselves, tell them you hate to see them suffering – point out how much they do to themselves that's unkind.

- Be sincere and speak from your own emotions.

Holy Virtue and Holy Idea:
Humility and freedom/will

The virtue of **humility** is mimicked by the pride that puts Twos at the service of others and denies their own needs. A person who experiences humility as a state of being knows and accepts their own nature, both strengths and weaknesses, and their real value to each person they encounter, whether fleetingly or in a long relationship. They can embrace the fact they are not always needed, and that they have needs of their own, without feeling diminished or unlovable; they can celebrate what they have to offer to the world.

Focusing their attention on the necessity, and ability, to flatter means that Twos surrender their **will**, and therefore their **freedom**, to others' agendas. Taking pride in their independence and emphasising freedom, in fact they are dependent. Real freedom is experienced by Twos when they follow their own highest will, which is born of Essence and the true needs of the moment, rather than an idea of 'I want' or 'I can give'.

Freedom/will is the knowing that whatever transpires is what is meant to, and so it makes sense to surrender to the will of now; and freedom comes when resistance to reality is let go. A **humble** heart knows its own true nature as part of the whole, and so expresses the truth of itself free from pretence.

Chapter 4

Type Three
The Performer

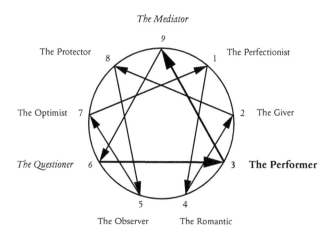

Outward appearance

Type Threes appear self-confident, ambitious, successful, fast-moving, workaholic, often charming and enthusiastic. They work hard in pursuit of their goals and can be good motivators, able to make others share their belief that anything is achievable. They can also appear unfeeling or manipulative in pursuit of their ends, and may unknowingly step on people in their single-minded focus on their goal.

Their life – including leisure time – seems to consist of a series of tasks to complete efficiently, goals to achieve, and they will start on the next before the current one is finished – 'down' time between goals would be wasted time. Mentally, they multi-task, holding two or more goals in mind and giving attention to each as needed. Attention to detail is not their strongest point. However, tasks will be successfully completed, even if corners are sometimes cut, since recognition for visible achievement is vital to them.

Threes appear competitive, since their focus is on winning, but they are quite likely to see themselves as accepting a challenge rather than trying to beat others.

> *'It wasn't until my sports teacher pointed it out that I realised my winning meant someone else losing. I really had no idea that me feeling great meant someone else feeling lousy. Inside I was competing with myself.'*

Performers rarely take risks, however, unless they have something to fall back on, and they only take on projects at which they feel they can succeed. Failure, if it happens, is redefined as 'partial success' or 'a learning experience', and they move on quickly to the next project. One of the most devastating things for Threes is a publicly witnessed failure.

Part of succeeding is to be liked by those whose approval matters, and, for Threes, that may be almost everyone. Although they are a heart type, their attention is not on feelings but on their image: other people's feelings in response to them.

With a fine-tuned intuitive awareness of other people's expectations, Threes can change their image, like a chameleon, to suit the people they are with. They can do this in a moment by changing their body language, and they can dress to be appropriate to any occasion. It is a very subtle process, which is often not noticed by people on the receiving end, and Threes themselves may not be aware of doing anything: *'I'm just able to get on with anybody.'*

Threes are disconnected from their own feelings. It is not that they *have* no emotions, but they postpone feeling them until they have time, and in their highly scheduled lives there is no time. Emotions can also threaten the image.

> *'Emotions interfere with getting the job done, and there is always a job to be done. If my husband asks me how I'm feeling, I really don't know. I'm too busy organising the family outing.'*

> *'I don't want to expose how I feel, so I distract myself into the task to be done.'*

In certain walks of life, particularly the caring professions or 'new age' circles, Threes can use their chameleon instinct to present appropriate feelings very convincingly, and may be genuinely surprised if self-exploration shows these are not always their true feelings.

Unaware Threes can be contemptuous, hard-nosed go-getters, dominating others for their own ends, with no access to feeling or human intimacy.

Aware Threes can be empathic, socially conscious leaders, able to enliven others with their own enthusiasm and hope, and capable of deep connection to people and worthy goals.

Inner concerns and childhood scenarios

Beneath the striving for success and recognition, Threes are in reality striving for love and acceptance for who they are. It seemed to them in childhood that only successful producers are loved, and therefore who they are, by itself, is not enough.

'Paradoxically, though I want her to say she will love and accept me as I am, even if I become a beer-swilling, football-watching couch potato, even if she said it, I wouldn't believe it. But I want her to say it, because if she has high expectations of me, I'd feel obliged to meet them. And then I'd always feel she only loves me for that, it's all a con, and if I stopped, she'd leave me. I know, in my head, that when she encourages me it's because she loves me – but it still feels as though I'll never be good enough. But she can't win either because I wouldn't believe it if she said I was.'

As children, Threes felt they had to do a lot, and do it well, to be loved or to feel worthy. Most remember being asked what they had achieved today, and what they were going to achieve tonight, next week, next month.

'They always asked me if I'd had a lovely day at school. The answer had to be "Yes", and then they asked what I'd done. But they never asked how I felt. I'd done a lot, so I must have had a lovely day.'

Some Threes recall their desire to succeed as driven by the need to escape from, be better than, a family or social group seen as inferior by the wider culture.

Passion and Fixation: Deceit and vanity/drive

The Passion of **deceit** does not mean Threes wilfully deceive others. First and foremost, they deceive themselves by identifying with the role(s) they have taken on. Since the need to be loved and accepted unconsciously underpins the drive to succeed, Threes select arenas, professional and social, that will gain the approval of the types of people they want to be accepted by.

They identify with their chosen roles, deceiving themselves that this is 'who they are', and may not even notice if these identities change over time. It may be as radical as a successful law student becoming an archetypal hippy, with everything implied in both lifestyles being successfully adopted.

Deceiving others is mainly a side-effect of this dynamic, coupled with Threes' ability to shift image. This is so subtle that they can be in a group of people and present themselves slightly differently to each person without it being noticed. For many Threes, this is unconscious; others are aware they can do it and see it as a useful skill.

> 'The image is the way I see myself as well as how others see me. It's not necessary to do what they're talking about, but to look as though I am, with the least possible trouble. Goals are important, but it all goes towards the image.'

Sometimes this strategy can fail, because they are so intent on their image they do not notice the effect they actually have. 'When I left I found out my nickname at work had been "Hitler". I was amazed – I was Mr Nice Guy.'

Threes begin to be sceptical about their identification when they become aware that they will bend the truth to maintain the facade of success.

> 'It may not be going great but you say it is because you know it will be great... Reality is relative to how I want it to be in the end. I miss so many cues because of this... You're fooling yourself, but you're fooling others too.'

Praise, too, normally welcome, may trigger scepticism about the validity of their image.

> 'There's an incongruity between the way you feel about something and the way you appear or behave around it. You smile and say "Thanks," but inside it's "But it's not me they're praising."'

Vanity lies in Threes' knowledge that they have the energy, the motivation and the skills (or the determination to acquire the skills) to succeed where others don't: *'I always believed everyone else was as ambitious as me, they just weren't so good at it. I still have a sneaking contempt for people who don't seem to want to succeed.'*

This is supported by their mental **drive** to keep 'doing'. They bring all their energy and motivation to an enterprise, and respond instantaneously to a challenge – *'At any moment I will move into gear...'* – taking charge and doing whatever needs to be done. They know they can succeed, and are frustrated by other people's approach.

> *'It's hard to stand back and let others do it for themselves because I can see how much more efficiently I would do it... I have to do it all... It feels like I have to take responsibility for the success of anything I'm involved in.'*

This feeds back into the vanity: *'If I'm honest, I like being seen as the "can do, will do" person.'*

Because of this focus of attention, Threes can work themselves into the ground. Energetically, there is no middle ground, and they only stop doing when they run out: *'My energy is either flat out or there's none left – I go into slob mode, can't even be bothered to shave.'*

Stress

> *'No matter what I do, I'm failing (in public!).'*

Threes thrive under what most of the rest of the world would call stress, but they *can* experience it: public failure, taking on far too much, illness which forces them to stop and inactivity are examples of stress for a Three.

They take on qualities of Nine, the Mediator, and start to lose their focus and with it their confidence. There may be a tendency to over-indulge with things like *'football, drink, drugs'*, and they become easily swayed or distracted, and upset that they can't seem to promote themselves well.

> *'I knew we had agreed what I was responsible for, it was mine to do, and I could do it. Then they started telling me not to do it that way, do it this way... Finally, they said I was insubordinate and not doing the job. I started wondering – whichever one I was talking to, I wondered if his was the way to do it. I really lost my self-confidence. Finally, I got angry, but when I tried to tell them, they talked me out of it.'*

> *'If I go in over my head – take on too much, don't have a plan or haven't done my research well enough – I just become paralysed.'*

Security

In the emotional security of, for example, a committed relationship, when there is no need for them to perform, Threes may begin to get in touch with their own feelings. This can feel frightening as they go to Six, the Questioner and the central fear type, in security.

It is also a Catch-22 situation: emotions are seen as threatening anyway because they interfere with the job; then, when Threes feel secure enough to access them, fear immediately comes up, confirming the idea that emotions are dangerous. This is one of the reasons they find it so hard to relax and do nothing: *'As long as I'm busy I don't have to go into the fear.'*

Doubt also arises, of themselves, the situation and their feelings. Threes on the path of self-discovery report that it takes them a long time to discover their true emotions.

> *'Is this a real feeling, or is it just another part of my image? It was very confusing for a long time. Learning to just sit still*

and "be" with my family was one of the hardest things I've ever had to do.'

Subtypes

The Passion of deceit is primarily about maintaining the feeling – and the demonstration – that *"who I am" is successful and therefore worthy of love'.*

Dissipating the raw energy and obscuring deceit from everyday consciousness, the subtype allows Threes not to have to face the possibility of the image being merely a self-deception.

Self-preservation: Security

In the area of self-preservation, Threes' attention focuses on material security. Success means having enough and to spare; and from this point of view there is never enough. The ultimate success is always in the future, with the achievement of yet another goal.

> *'I come from a poor background. It has been a lifelong determination that I would never be in those financial straits. I'm in venture capital, and although I have savings, property and an income others raise their eyebrows at, I can't seem to lose that feeling. It's actually a burden to me now, and I know it's irrational, but I have this inner compulsion to keep going so that I'm secure.'*

Social: Status and prestige

Threes who focus on social survival are concerned with their status in the group. Each goal is targeted for the potential prestige it will give them in their workplace and their community, and membership of a certain club may be as important a goal as success at work.

'I'm head of, or on the committee of, most of the good local organisations and social clubs. I'm regularly in the local paper for charity drives or gala openings – small pieces, but my community knows me, and knows that I know important people outside our local group. But also respect is important: I am known and liked – I always get a friendly greeting.'

Sexual: Masculine/feminine

For this subtype, the constant focus on image in general is overlaid and augmented by a need to appear absolutely masculine or feminine, depending on gender. These Threes are successful at being 'men' or 'women', at least in the eyes of the world.

'It's always been important to me that I look good, that people look at me and are attracted. It's not just sexual attraction, though going out to dinner I will dress elegantly and discreetly in the style I know my date likes. I look feminine, but I'm in business, and I'm usually the most sharply dressed "business man" there, and I do the job as a man would, if not better.'

Relationships

Although Threes are socially adept and can be entertaining and enlivening companions, relationships are a difficult area for them. Friendship in itself has no goal, and the prospect of just 'being' together, maybe for ever, can make them anxious and restless.

'It's almost as though relationships get in the way of getting things done. The trouble is, a relationship is not a concrete thing – there's no finished end product.'

At work, relationships are instrumental: they are about working together to get the job done. If it looks as though a working relationship is in trouble, Threes will fix it so they can get on, and while some are sensitive to people's response to them, some do not notice if others are upset. The image is 'Mr Nice Guy', though they may walk over someone to get to the goal, and *because I didn't want to share how I felt, people experienced me as cold, efficient, separate from them'.*

Personal relationships can also be instrumental in backing up the image, so for some Threes it is worth working hard at doing it right, finding out what they need to do to make it work. *'I look for my role in the relationship – when I find it, that's OK, I can do that.'*

This doesn't always work, however, if their partner wants more feeling and more 'being together'. Partners can feel disregarded in a social setting when their Three's attention is on the crowd and the image they are creating, and can feel they are not seen and valued for themselves, merely as an adjunct to the image.

If a relationship fits a Three's image, they may find it hard to understand if their partner is not satisfied.

> *'What do they want me to do? If she says she's unhappy, I'll go and do the washing up, buy flowers, put up a shelf… Just tell me what I've done – and what I have to do to put it right.'*

Threes bring energy, optimism and activity to intimate relationships, though even in a lifelong partnership they may always feel it *could* end, either because they are unlovable, or because they need a goal (a new successful relationship). Some avoid intimacy altogether.

> *'Relationships are very stressful for me. I choose specific people, and I can only handle so much intensity. It's much easier if we have things to do in common.'*

Things Threes can do to help themselves grow

- Stop from time to time and ask, 'What am I feeling?'

- Take time out to stop and be: go for walks (but without a goal!), stare at the sunset, learn to meditate for its own sake rather than as a task.

- Ask trusted friends to tell you when they feel you're not being real or you're fudging an issue, and listen even if they seem wrong.

- Notice yourself changing image to please, and ask yourself, 'Is this who I am or am I going for the image?'

- Pay attention to physical sensations, especially tiredness: slow down.

- Use physical sensations as clues to what you might be feeling.

- Notice yourself speeding or acting mechanically, your mind going to multiple tasks, postponing emotions: slow down.

- Use frustrations as a reminder to look around, rather than attacking the goal even harder or jumping to the next one.

- Work on valuing empathy and connection as highly as status.

- Acknowledge to yourself and be truthful about weakness and failures; feeling a fraud is a good sign.

- Ask yourself what really matters to you, in your work and leisure, and make time to pursue it.

- When people ask you to just hang out with them, remember it means they like you, and practise doing it.

Things friends can do to support Threes

- Encourage them in all of the above.

- Let them know you care for who they are aside from accomplishments, and that it's OK to feel vulnerable.

- Remember they look confident but they're not.

- Don't criticise or attack – it hurts and will increase low self-esteem, reinforcing the cycle.

- Don't reinforce achievement alone by praising results only.

- Support them in exploring their being: who they are.

- Let them know how you feel without needing a particular response.

- Remember that emotions are scary for Threes, and don't take it personally if they seem to back away when they start to feel.

- Stay steady in appreciating them, not their results.

Holy Virtue and Holy Idea: Honesty and hope

Honesty is an inner state in which there is no need to find a role to identify with. Rather than look to others to have their being validated, a person experiencing honesty knows that 'this is who and what I am, and this is enough'. They do not need to look outside and convince others, and so themselves, that they are lovable: they know it within themselves.

Hope in Essence is not, as it often is in its day-to-day meaning, a sort of wishing. The mental focus of vanity can be stated as 'I am the one who can – and therefore must and will – do it.' When Threes reach a state of awareness in which they know that Essence takes care of what needs to happen, there is holy hope. They are able to let go and allow things to be done through them rather than by them.

Threes who experience hope and honesty can turn their leading, achieving and motivating skills to the service of other people, and no longer striving for it, nor hidden behind an image, experience the unconditional love they have always longed for.

Hope perceives that existence is the creation of a benign reality unfolding as it should, giving a profound implicit hope that does not need to 'hope things go right'. **Honesty** gives a full immersion in the experience of who I am within the all, and thus I know and express myself as real.

Chapter 5

Type Four
The Romantic

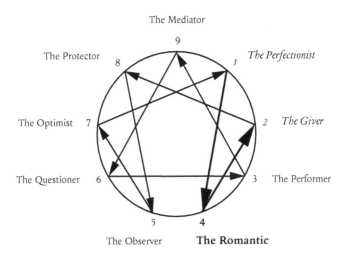

Outward appearance

Type Fours bring an intense and dramatic quality to life. The ultimate idealists, they refuse the mundane and are attracted to extremes of emotion and action. They seem to enjoy living on the edge and seek out the unusual, artistic and meaningful in all areas of life. What others might judge to be a morbid fascination with things such as death, suffering, birth and people's innermost feelings, they describe as valuing depth and authenticity.

They can be outgoing and flamboyant, and even reserved Fours draw the attention with their air of being special in some way. Aesthetically aware, their clothing and surroundings express their sense of uniqueness and need for beauty and significance. They can sometimes seem elitist and superior, as though other people cannot share their refined understanding.

Highly creative, and, from other types' point of view, over-emotional, Fours can be exhilarating to be around, but they can also be depressing or frustrating. They often seem attracted to the sad side of life, and a subtle sense of deficiency is coupled with their air of specialness, as though 'I – and it – can never be good enough.' They bypass ordinary feelings by setting up goals that are more or less impossible.

> 'I'm an actress and there's always a higher plane you can reach for. I push myself to be at every audition. My fantasy of success as an artist cannot be achieved by what I am now – I need to be better.'

Fours focus on relationship and feelings, so although they are idealistic about their work, the search for the ideal partner takes priority. Work can be rapidly, if temporarily, set aside if a new relationship appears or an existing one is in trouble.

Fours tend to relate in a push–pull way, except with trusted intimates. The more distant, the more perfect someone looks, whereas once they are close, their imperfections become obvious and they are pushed away, whereupon distance makes them attractive again. This creates a self-fulfilling prophecy of relationships not working.

Fours may seem to actively desire 'negative' emotions, and some are diagnosed as bipolar when they are simply an 'extreme' Four. When life is getting ordinary, or they suffer a seemingly small upset, they can create a crisis of emotion, becoming angry or more upset if anyone tries to reason them out of it or put things right.

> *'There's the enjoyment of the angst and the feeling I want to hold on to it, and if he can make me laugh, goddamn it, I won't be able to hold on to it – the energy's dissipated. So laughing does get me out of it – but I don't want to!'*

On the other hand, Fours are deeply and genuinely empathic with other people's suffering, and will instantly drop their own troubles to support and help someone in pain. Authenticity also matters a lot to them, so:

> *'I don't want to have the power to make it all terrible for everyone if I'm in a mood. Sometimes it's hard to tell if it's really serious or if I should drop it. It feels real, but I know I can work myself up over nothing.'*

Knowing, and expressing, the truth is very important to Fours: *'I want to know where I stand regardless of the cost. What upsets me most is being misunderstood – meaning something well and finding that's seen differently.'*

Unlike the other heart types, Fours are self-referencing. They are concerned with relationships and how they come across, but their image is an expression of themselves, and they seldom change to gain approval.

> *'I always know what decision I would make. In terms of daily things, or if I don't care much, I will ask him what he wants. But if I'm passionate about something, I just do it. It's hard to relinquish something I'm passionate about.'*

Unaware Fours can be moralistic, guilt-ridden, self-obsessed emotional manipulators, demanding attention for their pain and unwilling to admit either help or the idea that their emotions might be over-blown.

Aware Fours can be creative, charismatic and empathic people. Combining love of the spiritual in life with acceptance of the here and now, they may be superb artists and helpers of others in threshold situations: hospices, refugee camps, maternity wards.

Inner concerns and childhood scenarios

Fours' underlying feeling is that they were abandoned or somehow separated from the original source of unconditional love, and their attention focuses on seeking out the perfect love that will make them complete again.

This has a complementary belief that, to have been 'abandoned', they must have been unworthy. Their unconscious premise is 'I must be special and unique to attract and deserve the perfect love, but secretly I know I cannot deserve or keep it'.

> 'I always knew I was different. I was favoured by my mother, and I could never work out why I felt like a black sheep. Then I found my father was not my blood father, and started a quest to find him – and always feeling "Why did he let me go, why does he not claim me?"'

> 'Abandonment was not about a person but the divine, and no human could measure up to what I considered sacred. I've always been searching for the ultimate divine experience. I had been ripped away from something that was sacred; therefore ordinary everyday life would be pretty boring.'

Fours' reports of childhood vary – for example, a parent left or travelled a lot; they were adopted as babies; a twin died; they spent a lot of time in hospital; or their parents may simply have denied emotional connection.

The common thread is the depth and range of emotion they felt in compensation. Some Fours grew up feeling their emotions were part of what was wrong with them, and lost contact with them. For the majority of young Fours, feeling deep emotions is just the way it is, and yet they know they are different:

> *'I said I had more nerve endings than other people. Art was a way of getting it out. As an adult, I realise it's also self-validating – I felt there was something wrong with me, but "Look, I'm special, I have these emotions."'*

Passion and Fixation: Envy and melancholy

The passion of **envy** underlies Fours' sense of being inferior. Envy is not jealousy, but a constant sensation in the heart of something missing and a yearning to fill the emptiness. Fours seek completion, but it feels like trying to attain the unattainable: *'Disappointment is an overriding issue most of the time.'* Their attention focuses on what is missing, so what is present, because not fully experienced, is not good enough, thus confirming that something must be lacking.

Fours look around them and feel that if only they could have that particular thing, they would be all right. It can range from envying someone for an unusual piece of clothing, a character trait or nurturing parents, to beautiful surroundings, or imagining everyone else has the perfect relationship they can never have themselves.

Envy also fuels the highly individual elitism of the Four. Envying others, they do not seek to be like them but to express the unique and real in themselves. With a vivid image of what would fill the emptiness, they are refined in their choice of surroundings and ways of doing things. Sensitive to mood, they look for people who can share their sensitivity and their search for the meaningful.

> *'There was always the idealised image – in college I wrote a poem about all the girls I'd gone out with and there was always*

> *something wrong. I approached people and experiences with an idealised image rather than allowing the experience to be what it was. I had an idea of how I wanted it to be and then the experience had to measure up. That's been characteristic of a lot of things I've done.'*

The very intensity of the emotions involved helps Fours to feel authentic and worthwhile, making envy hard to satisfy; for if the longed-for ideal were to arrive, yearning would have to be sacrificed.

Melancholy is a mental focus that gives life a bitter-sweet flavour. Life is not about anything as trivial as happiness: when Fours experience joy, it is passionate and deep, but includes the knowledge that its opposite is never far away. They recognise and embrace the idea that true creativity and perfect love must be suffered for – in fact, are born of suffering.

Fours welcome deeply felt emotion as a source of creative energy. There is a clear dividing line for them between melancholy, which is a true and meaningful emotion, and depression, which may feel real at the time but is the result of being stuck in a negative loop.

> *'I can start over, create anew. It's self-expression – taking all that emotion and using it. Also, I don't get bored: it takes me from activity to activity on lots of different levels. I lose it when I get depressed. That's the difference between depression and melancholy: melancholy is part of the creative urge; depression destroys it.'*

Stress

> *'No matter what I do, my unique qualities...aren't good enough to get me the feeling of connection/completeness I crave.'*

The further Fours are from the ideal, the more they feel they need to change themselves in some way, whether in their creative life or in relationship, and the more stressful life becomes. As they take on characteristics of Two, the Giver, there is a dovetail with their characteristic push–pull way of relating, as they feel the need to attract people and be approved of.

> *'It's awful – I become such a toady. I go around asking people if there's anything I can do to help, anything. It's like I've got to find something to do to make me worthy in their eyes because unless I do something I'm no one. I stay after work, make all the tea and coffee, let people borrow my clothes, which I'd normally never do.'*

Security

Fours are idealists in the realm of feelings and the heartfelt living of life. When a relationship or their work goes well, and they start to feel emotionally validated and secure in themselves, they add another aspect of perfectionism to their personality. They take on qualities of One, the Perfectionist, and become critical of themselves and others, paradoxically (unconsciously) driving away the emotional well-being as soon as it arrives.

> *'I'm very nit-picking with [my partner] when I'm sure he loves me. Poor guy, no wonder he gets worried I'm about to leave – but actually it's because I care that I can't bear him to be less than his best. And I get really scared of abandonment, so I push him to find out. But I'm also hard on myself. That's the time I'm most likely to start another self-development course – so of course I'm not at home so much, so... It's probably a relief to him when I start to get insecure again, even with all the emotion.'*

Subtypes

The Passion of envy is paradoxically about fuelling the drive to prove lovability, in that it creates the sense of being lacking or flawed in some way, which then drives the insistence on authenticity. Unlike the other heart types, Two and Three, the Four does not change to gain approval. 'Since I am flawed, I must be authentic and unique to prove my worthiness of love – and yet everyone else seems to have the very thing(s) that are lacking in or for me.'

Dissipating the raw energy and obscuring envy from everyday consciousness, the subtype allows Fours not to have to face the actual experience of a fear of having no 'place' in the world, 'due to what I lack', and masking it with the sense that 'at least I am authentic, unique and sensitive'.

Self-preservation: Reckless / dauntless

Envy is kept at bay in the realm of self-preservation by taking risks and living life recklessly. To really be alive means to experience life to the full, to be extraordinary and willing to take whatever comes along and dauntlessly ride with it. To be safe in a predictable world is life-denying.

> *'To be ordinary is death – I literally feel I will die – so I keep myself alive by breaking the rules. I combat the envy this way: it makes me unique. It's also an escape from loneliness and sorrow to up the ante on my own sense of being alive.'*

Social: Shame

Envy expresses itself in the social arena with a sense of shame, of not being good enough, and a fear that people will notice this and reject the Four. They deal with this by applying creativity to their involvement in the group, making wonderful hosts or hostesses, or the one who makes sure an event – social or business – is really special.

'Shame can be a motivator, to cover up the deficiencies by being involved. However, this has been a cover for me not expressing my own identity and needs in case they don't measure up.'

Sexual: Competition / hate

In one-to-one relationships, Fours can become competitive, both with a third party and with the friend or partner. Envy is displaced into hatred of whatever threatens to show up their own shortcomings. It can sometimes take the form of competing with themselves against their inner ideal, and knowing they are bound to lose. For Fours who don't see themselves as competitive in the world, it can be recognised as a constant need to 'have the last word' in discussion.

'Competition is a form of envy: my self-referencing attention inside me comparing "Do I have that, am I that good?" with women. Strangely, if a woman is very unlike me, she's not a threat, probably because she's not likely to displace me. And with men it's rage at having surrendered my whole being. I'm trying to prove I'm equal.'

Relationships

Even though relationships are central in Fours' lives, friends and particularly partners may find it hard to know exactly how to relate to them. Fours' emotional experience can vary so widely and so intensely that, coupled with their push–pull habit, it may be hard for them and others to know where they stand.

If they are in any doubt about a friendship, they become cautious and pull back. They need to know a person is there for them, values them and is willing to pay attention and validate their feelings. Even in a committed friendship, they may not verbalise how they feel, but express themselves through their mood. *'I want you to see something's wrong, but I won't tell you – I want to know, are you paying attention to me, are you there for me?'*

Push–pull is less likely to operate in a friendship than in an intimate relationship. They appreciate people who will match their intensity and share their awareness of the meaningful and romantic. When they feel they have found a real friend, they are loyal and generous.

> *'I have as much pleasure in doing it for someone else as having it done for me – creating the unique, the wonderful, the special – even if it's just a home-made birthday card.'*

Relationships, as well as feelings, can be inflated by Fours' imagination.

> *'I'm looking for the real – authenticity – but I live in a world of fantasy. Often relationships are mostly in the head – between one meeting and another I've had so many interactions, which seemed absolutely real, that we're completely out of synch. I know we've had deep and meaningful conversations; for her, I'm still just someone she met at a party last week.'*

Partners in intimate relationships can feel they are trying to measure up to what is expected and often failing. Fours project their original abandonment on to all relationships, and can push their partner away if the going gets even a little tough or they foresee rejection.

> *'I want to be the one who leaves rather than the one who is abandoned. If I feel I don't have control, it's really scary.'*

Fours appreciate unique, interesting gestures which keep the relationship special and show that their uniqueness is seen and valued – small, unusual gifts or events planned specially for them. For many Fours, romance is already all-pervading in their lives, and they are touched and reassured by anything that is for them alone.

'The way my daughter moves across the floor, the look on his face when he's watching her, the birds in the garden, all create a romantic cloud I live my life in. A dinner won't do it because my day is already romantic. But the cake the two of them made together…'

Things Fours can do to help themselves grow

- Take up a body-based activity to learn to ground yourself.

- When your emotions become very strong about something, question them by tracking back to the first feeling which triggered them: it may be different to what you feel now.

- Notice your attention going to what is missing, and learn to value the positive aspects of what is here and now.

- Remind yourself that 'abandonment' was in the past and is not inevitable.

- Find something positive to celebrate every day.

- Start to value and enjoy the mundane: see the extraordinary in the ordinary.

- Recognise specialness and self-absorption as a way of masking fears of abandonment: focus on what is important to someone else.

- Set up structures in your daily life that help you stay consistent when the feelings start to build, and to complete things that will benefit you.

- Notice when your strong feelings make you feel special and right: take time to consider before acting on them.

- Notice sarcasm and anger as a way of blaming others for your suffering, and thus perpetuating it because 'it's not my fault'.

- Discover the qualities in yourself that you envy in others.

- Honour your own idealism and your ability to empathise with others' pain, without getting attached to them.

Things friends can do to support Fours

- Support them in all of the above.

- Be solid, consistent, reliable: let them know you won't abandon them.

- Don't try to 'fix it' for them – do not give advice or try to talk them out of it.

- Be there for them, listen to their feelings and believe them – but don't 'buy into' it; just acknowledge its reality for them.

- Give them space – let them have their emotions and work through them.

- Tell them your own feelings and reactions.

- Appreciate their idealism and authenticity.

Holy Virtue and Holy Idea:
Equanimity and origin

Equanimity is the experience of being harmonious and complete in oneself in the midst of any experience. The habit of envy places the source of completion outside the self. Fours who reattain equanimity realise they already have everything they need within themselves as people, and have a genuinely important place in life by virtue of who they innately are. They are able to stay balanced, not needing to lose themselves in intense experiences as a way of proving their worth.

Along with this is the realisation that they have never lost connection with Essence. Melancholy because they feel abandoned, Fours feel they must seek out perfect or divine love, the creative source. Once they look inside, they find they are part of the **holy origin**, and are able to celebrate and let that creative source express itself through them in their lives.

Origin is the understanding that we as individual souls, as well as all creation, are part of the loving Being, which is in fact our ground of being, our very nature. The attitude of **equanimity**, knowing my own wholeness, does not value one thing over another, but receives and rejoices in whatever comes.

Chapter 6

Type Five

The Observer

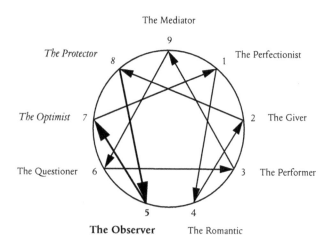

Outward appearance

Type Fives tend to seem withdrawn, intellectual, focused, quiet, objective and unemotional, knowledgeable yet unforthcoming, and self-sufficient. They are fear types who present themselves as distanced rather than afraid.

Most at home in the analytic realms of the mind, they often describe themselves as 'information junkies'. They enjoy facts and systems, and may have many interests or devote their intellect to an esoteric subject understood by only a few people in the world.

Fives are very private people, easily drained by too much interaction with others, sometimes even by another's presence nearby. They fear intrusion and need to have their own clearly acknowledged space, so they can retire to recoup their energy and think things through. This can range from a separate building to their own armchair:

> *'My kids know that when I come home Dad sits in his special chair for half an hour and is not disturbed. After that I'm happy to play or whatever, but I must have that space.'*

Because they experience everyday life as observers, at one remove from themselves and events, they cannot easily identify what they feel and think in the moment. They need privacy partially to review past and future events, and what they think and feel. If asked how they feel, or even for a business decision, Fives need to be allowed to go away and consider before they can give an accurate answer.

> *'If I'm with people and I feel that there's an expectation or I'm being watched for a reaction, I'm gone – not physically, but the ability to respond at all is just gone.'*

One way they may deal with the demands of new situations is to strike a pose and act a part: *'I have this wardrobe of characters in my head and put them on and off like suits.'*

Fives also compartmentalise their lives. Activities and interests each have their place, with time allotted, and seldom overlap. Business acquaintances are not friends and vice versa; different friends are associated with different activities. This is a protective measure which can make them seem secretive when they are simply maintaining their boundaries.

> *'Concentration on the one thing being done now is very clear – it feels natural to have the sectors of life separate.'*

They like to be able to anticipate and prepare themselves, and are rarely spontaneous: *'You may be one of my closest friends, but if you just knock on my door, my instinct is to tell you to go away.'* This may make them seem rigid, but they also prefer life not to be too predictable: *'Thursday evening debating club, every week, ad nauseam – ugh!'*

Methodical and consistent, if a Five says something will happen, it will. However, in work or on a joint project, they are happiest working independently in special knowledge areas. Having agreed to take something on, they want to be allowed to plan and execute it alone.

Fives can seem superior, which may simply be detachment, but may also be based in a belief that not only do they have more knowledge than most people, they also have a deeper insight and see clearly through things.

> *'It seems so grandiose, but I really do believe that I see things differently to other people, more accurately... I have a complete overview.'*

Fives have a minimalist lifestyle, needing very little to get by. Their shelves and refrigerators are rarely full, they travel light and they have few possessions – with one exception. In an otherwise bare room, they may have a full collection of items, often, but not always, related to their deepest interest, and ranging from photographic equipment or esoteric comic books to stones from beaches around the world.

Unaware Fives can be withdrawn, distrustful, critical, intellectually arrogant, unable to commit to anything, very controlled and out of touch with feelings and the world.

Aware Fives can be sensitive, perceptive, dedicated, objective and creative thinkers, who can combine their sensitivity and analytic skills to be wise rather than knowing.

Inner concerns and childhood scenarios

Fives learnt that it was possible to be safe in an intrusive world where their very survival felt threatened, by withdrawing into their minds and becoming self-sufficient. They minimised hurt by distancing from sensations and emotions, and, unable to escape physically, they could become untouchable by being a spectator of events in their own lives.

> *'It can feel as though I'm looking over my own shoulder, or down on things from above. Sometimes, if I'm really gone, I can watch myself watching myself watching myself at three or four removes.'*

As children, they may have had intrusive, domineering, violent or smothering parents. They recall, for example, having their favourite toys destroyed *'because we haven't got room for them'*; or:

> *'I would escape to my room to read, but always within, it must have been, five minutes she'd yell up at me, and I could feel myself go cold and clenched inside, my heart would skip a beat, and then I'd turn into a robot. I would just move the feelings away. It's protective.'*

Some Fives, rather than feeling threatened by people, felt their survival threatened because they were left to fend for themselves.

> *'I never knew when the next meal would be, so I just decided that's OK, I don't need food to survive.'*

Passion and Fixation: Avarice and stinginess

Avarice is an emotional preoccupation, in which Fives feel they are always potentially lacking the means for safe survival, and so are avaricious of whatever enables them to feel secure and independent. This is not usually anything material, as they minimise physical needs, but information that enriches their inner world and helps them feel prepared for the onslaughts of the outer world.

> *'If I were to be shipwrecked, or if some kind of disaster happened, I know I'd survive where other people wouldn't. For one thing, I can get by on very little; in fact, I enjoy not having too much – otherwise I feel weighed down and trapped – but, also, I've read all the survival manuals. Specially nowadays, it seems to make sense…'*

They also feel an intense need – a sort of greed – for private space and time, both for safety's sake and for nourishment.

> *'Independence is a preoccupation – something I value a lot. The inner world is self-sustaining, I could live by myself and survive. There were occasions when I felt lonely, but by and large it was enjoyable. The privacy is actually nourishing. I love being alone with no demands on me at all – it's ecstasy.'*

Stinginess with necessities is natural when they might be taken away at any moment. For Fives, the greatest necessities are time, energy and personal space. Alert and observant, like all head types, they are particularly responsive to nuances in another's presentation. If other people make demands on them (and almost any request can seem like a demand), they will respond calmly, but *'though I can give what they need, I give it just enough so they go away again'.*

> *'My knee-jerk reaction when people asked me how I was, was "I'm fine" – I didn't give a lot, so people just left me alone.'*

Although most Fives are knowledgeable about many varied subjects, they tend not to volunteer information unless asked, even when it would be useful. There is nothing malicious in this; it is simply safer to give out as little as possible. They may feel their information is inadequate, and it does not occur to them that other people might be interested in what they have to say. They may also feel that to give out information, or share their creativity, is to give away something of themselves.

Similarly, in social situations or business meetings, if the agenda isn't clear, their instinct is to retreat and review. Feeling that personal energy is strictly limited, they fear being drained by unexpected demands and interactions.

> *'There's a risk I'll be swept up into something I'm not prepared for and haven't got an intellectual answer for... There's a real sense of danger even in minor spontaneous events like being pulled out to a party. I have to assess my availability, what's wanted and what I can give.'*

Stress

> *'No matter what I do, they still keep coming after me/into my space.'*

Anything that forces Fives to deal with feelings or be immediate can be stressful. As the fear of being overwhelmed increases (and fear itself is a feeling they normally block out), they become more like Seven, the Optimist. However, it's not the actual optimism they adopt, just the appearance. Scanning for all possible escape strategies, they are unwilling to commit themselves to any, and may appear scattered.

> *'I'll strike a pose and become Sevenish and cheerful and gregarious – but actually I'm miles away. I start to scan mentally for all the possibilities of what might happen, and also look for all the options of escape for me, so I'm prepared for all the possible situations.'*

Security

When they feel emotionally secure, Fives become more Eight-like (the Protector). They can take charge, are definite and forthcoming, and access their anger. Protective of family members, they can also seem bossy. Normally, they find it easiest to express feelings through touch, and this is enhanced in security with a release of physical enjoyment. Type Eight qualities can also be seen in the quiet vigour with which Fives protect their own space or stand up for causes they care about.

> *'Friends who have only met us at parties, for example, say they get quite a shock if we invite them into our home. She's so much the outgoing powerful one, and then at home they hear me going, "Do this, do that, have another drink..." Mind you, by the time anyone gets to come back to the house the first time, I'm pretty damn sure they're lifelong friends.'*

Subtypes

The Passion of avarice is primarily about maintaining a sense of security and ability to survive in a chaotic and unpredictable world. Avarice is not greed; it is about assuring the necessities for life are available – private time and space.

Dissipating the raw energy and obscuring avarice from everyday consciousness, the subtype allows Fives to be assured that the world cannot take away their means of survival: with minimal needs, well informed and with withdrawal strategies firmly in place, they need not confront the fear that underlies their type.

Self-preservation: Castle

Fives experience avarice in the area of survival as 'my home is my castle'. Attention is focused on the home and creating a warm, secure place where they have all they need. Its expression can range from solitary living to being the dedicated home-maker in a relationship.

> *"Castle" speaks for itself. I live in a cottage at the end of a track, which I'm renovating. There are trees around it, but I can see right down the track from most of the rooms. I have a phone, but I always let the answering machine answer it. I can't remember the last time I invited anyone to my house. When I do, it's a really big thing for me: it means I trust you absolutely and I want your friendship; but it still feels worrying.'*

Social: Totems

Social avarice involves the 'collection' of totem figures: that is, knowing people who have symbolic importance in society or the chosen social group. In this way Fives feel safe in the group because they have direct access to the key source of information and control. It may also involve totemic information: understanding the key or esoteric system(s) that govern social interactions – for example, the Enneagram.

> *'In any group – well, take this one. I've had almost no contact with you or the other leader, but if I'm honest with myself, I want it. But I don't do it because I might be rejected. Even saying this is an oblique way of making that connection with minimum risk because now you know I want it, but I've said it in the context of contributing to the group, and we could both pretend that was my only motive for saying it.'*

Sexual: Confidences

The exchange of confidences in one-to-one relationships enables Fives to feel safe. Sharing secrets keeps the world at bay and means people trust each other, so Fives need not fear intrusion or loss. There is also a confidentiality in the physical expression of friendship or love that feels safer than verbal expression.

> *'I see it as giving away the burden of my secrets. If I give her my secrets, I trust her. I have an image of myself as a hunchback: the humps are my secrets. I used to tell people half-truths (not lies, but not all the truth). Now I'm learning to give it all away – it serves me, and my integrity, to be seen, and if the people I care for accept them and me, then I'm OK.'*

> *'If I can touch you, I know you; and a touch is truer, more complete, less demanding and more immediate than words – for a moment or two I can let myself experience now, and I don't have to hold myself back. That's blissful.'*

Relationships

Fives know they are distanced from the world and crave connection, but since it means making themselves vulnerable to feelings, and carries the risk of intrusion, it can be difficult for them.

However much they may like another person, anything experienced as invasive or demanding will make them back off, whereas they will be attracted towards a person who allows them their own space. When this is present, they feel an immense and safe latitude for give and take.

They also like an informed connection: they need to know who a person is and feel able to support them. They tend to select friends who share common interests, and relate at first on the level of shared activities. Fives are aware of, and deprecate, their own lack of spontaneity, and once they decide that connection is more important than safety, start to enjoy a structured letting-go.

'I've got involved in improvisational acting recently and it's helped a lot – it's made me more spontaneous. I think on my feet and get involved with people – it's really exciting.'

As a friendship becomes more intimate, non-verbal aspects of relationship are important. Touching allows them to feel present without the need to say how they feel, which they often do not know until they are alone. The reliable presence and consistency of another person allows them to feel safe.

Successful intimate relationship depends on partners understanding and respecting Fives' need for privacy:

'Even the cats know not to go into his room. If I knock on the door and he invites me in, they come as far as the doorstep but no further. He wasn't cruel or anything – it's just so obviously forbidden territory.'

And their dislike of being at the centre of attention:

'I need to feel I can be on my own when I need to be, without feeling I'm losing the relationship. For example, when we're driving, she will sleep or read, so the attention's off me but she is there.'

If these needs are met, intimate relationship can bring Fives out of themselves and extend their horizons.

'Until I got married at 39, I never thought marriage would work for me – I needed so much space for myself. But it's a link to the outside world, and to particular and very important needs in myself.'

Partners also need to understand that although Fives may be undemonstrative, and may appear to have the relationship in just one of their compartments, once they commit themselves, the relationship is central and probably the most important fact in their lives.

Things Fives can do to help themselves grow

- Take up a physical practice to help you ground in your body.

- Join a group that encourages self-disclosure – for example, gestalt, Narrative Tradition Enneagram workshops.

- Allow yourself to feel physical sensations and emotions whilst they are happening.

- Recognise, experience and recall pleasant feelings: realise that not all feelings are painful.

- If you meditate, become aware of the difference between detachment (watching yourself) and non-attachment (nobody watching).

- Notice how your mind detaches from feelings and sorts things into compartments, and how secrecy and superiority create separation.

- Cultivate here-and-now behaviour, particularly allowing yourself luxuries.

- Behave as though there is more than enough to go round.

- If you are a collector, practise restraining your need for the next item, and discover other pleasures.

- Notice when you are controlling your space/time/energy and manipulating others through restricting what and when you will give: start to allow the control to drop.

- Observe how withdrawal can often cause people to intrude further: start to stand your ground.

- Learn to let yourself be seen: not just who you are but what you do.

Things friends can do to support Fives

- Encourage them in all of the above.

- Respect their need for privacy and don't take it as rejection.

- Be consistent in your friendship without intruding.

- Encourage here-and-now activities.

- Encourage gradual experience of feelings: tell them your own in a gentle manner.

- When encouraging them to act differently, use invitation rather than demand.

- Beware of over-intellectualisation and discussion of growth rather than action.

Holy Virtue and Holy Idea:
Non-attachment and omniscience

A possible pitfall for Fives in their personal growth is confusing detachment, which comes easily to them, with the higher awareness of non-attachment. **Non-attachment** allows feelings, experiences and things to come and go, knowing that the universe is abundant. Fives try to recreate the feeling of sufficiency by pulling in and holding on to the necessities for survival. Detachment is a way of holding back and enables them to deny that they care about things and are attached. As they start to allow their energy to flow more freely and share it with other people, they discover that it is self-renewing. They also discover how much they have been attached to their necessities. The inner knowing that they will be taken care of by life itself gives a simultaneous ability to be involved and yet to let go.

Omniscience is the experience of essential mind in which all knowing is available without the need to think or accumulate knowledge. Fives pacify their unacknowledged fears by acquiring information. As their personal growth takes them more into the realm of immediate experience and non-attachment to their personality, they discover they have access to wisdoms other than that of the intellect. Safety is found in an inner experience of already knowing all they need to know.

Omniscience sees reality as the Divine sees it: as one thing, with nothing left out and everything in its right place – it fits together perfectly and all is held and contained within it. **Non-attachment** gives and receives freely, as the natural movement of the heart in a world where nothing is lacking is outwards.

Chapter 7

Type Six
The Questioner

The Mediator

9

The Protector 8

The Perfectionist 1

The Optimist 7

2 The Giver

The Questioner 6

3 The Performer

5 4

The Observer   The Romantic

Outward appearance

Type Sixes are usually loyal, hard-working, dependable, cautious and imaginative thinkers. More often team players than leaders, they can nevertheless put themselves on the line on behalf of downtrodden and unfairly treated people.

Sixes distrust authority and avoid being subject to authority figures, though they may hope, often unconsciously, to find a trustworthy leader, and some actively seek the security of an authority they need not question.

The Six personality manifests in many ways, from the timid to the confrontational. They can be difficult to recognise as 'fear' types and often do not see themselves as fearful. The hallmark of their type is a doubting frame of mind that questions their own decisions, others' motives and the safety of any situation.

> *'We're not scaredy-cats – it's not the kind of fear you read about in children's books. I don't see myself as fearful – but doubt and scanning, yes, I do that.'*

They make good trouble-shooters, as they automatically imagine the worst possible outcomes in any situation and ways to deal with them. For Sixes, this is intelligent thinking and they can get irritated with people who do not plan to avoid disaster, or who see them as doom-mongers. They simply want to be prepared, but often seem over-prepared to other types.

As head-based types, their imagination has the power of reality. Worst-case scenarios are lived through in the head to the extent that fear can be dispelled 'because it's already happened'. If real danger threatens, Sixes deal with it promptly, calmly and effectively, and can seem very courageous. They can also show these qualities when defending the underdog: their own fears are irrelevant. *'I don't see it as courage – it just needs to be done.'*

They are good facilitators, for they see the undeveloped potential in other people and enjoy helping them bring it out. In fact, most requests for assistance will get a positive response from a Questioner.

However, Sixes avoid being in authority and find success hard to handle. Friends may be surprised to find them changing careers just when they were near the top, or having avoidable 'mishaps' when successful completion is near.

'I was in line for a management position, and one day I broke an unwritten rule. I was bumped downstairs as fast as they could! I can't say I didn't know what I was doing (though at the time it just seemed like the right thing to do), so I have to recognise I was deliberately shooting myself in the foot!'

They also find success hard to remember: their attention is on what might go wrong, so they tend to remember what *went* wrong. This compounds their predicament of self-doubt. Sixes question everything, including their own abilities, and so action is often replaced by thinking and procrastination.

Alert for hidden agendas, Sixes can be convinced that *'I know what you are really thinking – I can see what you are hiding and how you perceive the world.'* While they often do have genuine insight into the subtleties and probable outcomes of situations, this belief can lead them into false assumptions and projections about other people.

Emotionally guarded, Sixes find it uncomfortable to be affected by others and hard to receive compliments without wondering what the motive is beneath them. They can seem hard to approach, or pull back just when another person feels they are becoming close.

Unaware Sixes can be paranoid, ineffective, inflexible, unable to relate and have difficulty getting started or completing things. They can be either withdrawn, inactive and compliant, or potential delinquents.

Aware Sixes can be productive and imaginative with a fine discriminating mind, committed and protective friends and co-workers, and able to take a positive stand against harmful authority.

Inner concerns and childhood scenarios

Sixes decided early in life that the world is threatening and potentially damaging. Wanting to be safe, their focus turned to scanning for clues to potential threat, vigilance, doubting the obvious and a strong imagination.

Most commonly, Sixes report a genuinely threatening environment as children – for example, violence in the family or a mentally unstable or addictive parent who might change from love to anger at any moment.

> *'My mother used to tell me my father loved me – but he would beat me for doing something I thought was good or hit me at table for bad manners – so, don't tell me you love me because I don't believe you.'*

> *'What can you count on? I never felt I belonged because there was nothing I could trust. I could almost smell what mood my mother was in before I got in the door. If you can't count on the people you're supposed to belong to, how can you feel you belong?'*

Sometimes Sixes learnt fear from the environment:

> *'My parents had been refugees and we lived in a kind of ghetto, and we were a racial minority in that ghetto. I loved them very much and learnt to fear and despise authority on their behalf.'*

Passion and Fixation: Fear/doubt and cowardice

Doubt, rather than overt fear, is what defines Sixes. It is natural to feel doubtful of the trustworthiness of anything when there is a constant feeling of imminent threat. Doubt also masks fear by allowing Sixes to feel that, since everything is doubtful, the probability of negative outcomes is real.

Sixes are hypervigilant, scanning for sources of possible threat. Their senses are acute, even able to tune in to separate conversations in a crowded room. Mentally, they question situations, what others say and their own thoughts, and they focus on the future, imagining worst possible outcomes in an attempt to feel safe.

Alertness and an adrenaline high are part of fear. Sixes often say they enjoy their habitual state and do not want to lose the fear because they would lose the energy.

The two classic responses to fear – fight or flight – result in two types of Sixes. Some use both responses, depending on circumstances, but many lean to one or the other.

'Counter-phobic' (fight) Sixes pre-empt fear by confronting danger and going toward it: *'I get my retaliation in first.'* These people, men or women, can be aggressive and independent, and seem afraid of nothing. Their snarl, however, is that of a creature at bay, not a predator.

> *'A Kiwi man has to be macho – sports, drinking, fighting. I was in there with all the rest, more so. I just couldn't have ponced around going, "I'm scared." Actually, I'm terrified most of the time, though I only realised it recently.'*

'Phobic' Sixes prefer 'flight'. They are usually aware of their fear and avoid potentially harmful situations. Unassertive, even timid, it is phobic Sixes who are most likely to consciously avoid success (as opposed to just switching careers for fun) as it gives a high profile and is therefore dangerous.

> *'I found myself a niche – literally, in a corner – and sat there and got on with things, even when I disagreed with how I was being asked to do them.'*

They are also the most likely to seek out and follow an authority whom they judge to be trustworthy, with the danger that in their search for safety they may project 'good' qualities on to unworthy leaders.

Cowardice is a facet of the imagination, rather than unwillingness to face things. Shakespeare expressed the mental focus of anticipating a negative outcome: 'Cowards die many times before their deaths...' (*Julius Caesar*), and Sixes confront the day-to-day equivalents of death almost constantly in their minds.

Their behaviour is rarely 'cowardly', but this mental focus underlies procrastination, projection of imagined feelings on to others, intense curiosity and the need to remain unaffected and in control of their environment.

Sixes debate things, not only mentally but while obtaining information. Often excellent conversationalists (which is also a way of staying in control of situations), they easily take up the devil's advocate role. They like to qualify and explore the doubtful edges of things, and may take up an opposing stance just for fun as well as to clarify things.

> 'You pointed out yesterday that I say "but" a lot. Well, yes... but isn't that just because I want to find out the answers?'

Stress

> 'No matter what I do, I can't seem to get certainty/authority on anything.'

Under stress, Sixes move to the Performer and take on Three-like qualities. Many enjoy the feeling of 'kicking into gear' and reduced anxiety. They can deal with success more easily, stop procrastinating and apply their imagination to getting the job done. They also become more image-conscious and able to promote themselves. However, like Threes, they may work themselves into illness, and this stance reinforces their distance from emotion.

Some Sixes seem to like to keep themselves in stress as a way of escaping the fear and doubt.

> 'I often work on things at midnight before the deadline. But I do a very good job, and I do get results when someone's relying

on me for them. Funnily enough, it's when I'm on the road four days out of seven and I've my son's childminding to organise and the laundry and a high-powered conference to lead that I'm most effective. I haven't time to worry, and I need to be together and look the part and do the job I'm paid for, and I do. And I sort out the domestic stuff that usually has me in a swivet.'

Security

Once Sixes allow themselves to feel emotionally secure for a while, they become soft, warm and loving, or long to make connection. Like Nine, the Mediator, they are able to just 'be' with friends and loved ones, and enjoy the respite from vigilance and questioning. Paradoxically, it is not comfortable for long, since fear is rearoused by the unsafety of not doubting. Since Nine is a non-initiating type, long periods of emotional security can reinforce Sixes' tendency to inaction.

'I love being with my family and just doing what we feel like. Sunday morning with a huge breakfast and the papers and nothing to do is sacrosanct to me. But by Sunday evening I'll be in my study and I may be up nearly all night finishing off the things that need to be done. My wife found it very hard for a long time to reconcile Sunday morning with Sunday evening.'

Subtypes

Though many Sixes would not recognise themselves as fearful, even doubt has the strength of fear behind it. The Passion named fear/doubt is about staying emotionally alert to danger – even unlikely danger – in an unsafe world.

Dissipating the raw energy and obscuring fear/doubt from everyday consciousness, the subtype allows Sixes not to have to face the emotional 'belief' (i.e. fear) that all situations and relationships contain a possible threat in the face of which I could be helpless.

Self-preservation: Warmth / affection

Sixes handle fear in the area of survival by disarming potential hostility, being warm, giving, affectionate and personally loyal. Although this is seemingly enacted in the social arena, it is a way of dealing with concern for security and personal survival: 'If you like me, I needn't fear you, and you might help me keep my world safe.'

> *'I like to join groups and I like to give to my friends, and have fun together. It gives me a feeling of belonging, which makes me feel secure. If I think someone has betrayed me, I will usually try to work it out, even though it may hurt a lot at the time.'*

Social: Duty

This manifests as loyalty to the group and desire to ally with a socially worthy group and actively support it. Family ties are important, even when maintaining them is not always easy or pleasant. Usually, the focus is upon underprivileged or otherwise deserving groups, to whose cause the Six is dutiful: 'If I am serving the group well, it will support me in turn.' For most 'duty' Sixes, the word itself has good connotations, though they recognise they can run themselves ragged with the number of committees and group projects they take on.

> *'My father brought us up to be leaders, and leaders have responsibilities. Some of my siblings were rebels, but I studied hard, got good grades, didn't cause trouble and spent my holidays co-leading holiday camps for poor children. I enjoy putting my skills to the benefit of the group, particularly those*

where I'm improving things for the underprivileged. I have a hard time admitting it to myself, but my father's opinion of what I do still affects me. I consciously decided not to be a "leader", but I still sometimes wonder whether I should have been, whether it's some sort of betrayal not to use my brains, as he would say, "to the full".'

Sexual: Strength / beauty

The instinct of sexual subtype Sixes is to affect others so as not to be affected. They do this through strength and/or attractiveness. Strength may be in the unswerving service to a cause, or in personal 'courageous' behaviour – skydiving, motorcycle rallying and so on. Doubtful of their own attractiveness, Sixes may focus on a shared love of beauty or on making their surroundings beautiful.

'I used to think I was a Three, because if something needed to be done, I would just go out there and do it. People said I was courageous, but I didn't see it that way. I could act the part as well – put on the make-up, attract people to the cause and to me. I had several fairly long-term relationships, and I could certainly be strong for and on behalf of my partners, but the irony was that I was so determined not to be dependent that I lost what I now realise I was looking for – the intimacy of an equal relationship.'

Relationships

In friendship as well as intimate relationships, Sixes look for someone they can trust and with whom they can feel united against the (threatening) world. They need to feel they 'know' friends and partners, so they may ask questions without saying much about themselves, until they are sure they can trust.

They express friendship and love through actions, working alongside and supporting the other person. They enjoy intellectual involvement and generate many good ideas, so it can be frustrating that Sixes tend not to initiate things and prefer their partners to take the lead.

> *'I express emotionality through my loyalty, through my putting you first. When you win, it feels like it happens to me – it's that powerful. I'm not the object of attention, we did this together, and I can be selfless. I like that.'*

It is difficult, and frightening, for them to access their emotions. They feel safer if they have some control in the situation.

> *'It is terrifying when someone matters to me – them, not the things we do together. If I opened myself up to them, and they were to die or go away, I would be devastated – and that angers me.'*

In intimate relationships, it can be years before Sixes allow themselves to realise they are emotionally involved.

> *'It was about seven years into the relationship before I got in touch with my feelings in it. Then I knew why – it was frightening. At last these emotions were coming up towards the woman I loved – but, gods, it changed my whole vision and the way I think and the way I deal with life.'*

Even when Sixes are in love and have been committed for many years, doubt continues to arise. This can be confusing for partners, who may not realise the very expression of it is an expression of loyalty.

> *'Love is there, commitment is there. Doubt will come, but if I'm committed, I'll stay anyway. Love is very strong and immediate and threatening, so you have to escape into your head. While you're doubting, you may not feel love, but the beauty is if you*

don't feel it now, but you know you're going to stay, you know the love will return. I'm here for life, and my mind comes and goes on it. You know, love is much bigger than feelings!'

Things Sixes can do to help themselves grow

- Take up a physical practice to help bring your awareness into your body and out of your head; notice physical tension and being braced to face the worse, and relax.

- Be cautious of growth methods that are intellectually based: balance them with the physical.

- Notice when paranoid thoughts and projections arise, and ask yourself what's behind them.

- Ask yourself from time to time, 'Am I imagining this? Is it a genuine intuition or a projection?'

- Ask friends for feedback and a reality check: 'This is what I think is going on... Is it real?'

- Take time to remember and enjoy past successes and skills, and congratulate yourself on present ones.

- Notice how doubt shuts out relationships ('Can I trust them?'), and practise trusting and having faith.

- Notice when you give power away, and practise becoming your own authority.

- Notice when you question authority rather than looking for points of agreement.

- Accept your doubts and ambivalence: practise making choices and acting on them.

- Notice when thinking replaces action; learn to notice and trust your gut reactions.

- Use your imagination to create pleasant options; also to project threatening scenarios to the improbable limit so you can defuse and laugh at them.

- Counter-phobic Sixes: before going into action, ask yourself if it is appropriate, and whether you have anything to prove.

Things friends can do to support Sixes

- Encourage them in all of the above.

- Remind them of pleasant alternatives to offset the negative ones: help them trust the future.

- Encourage them to initiate positive action.

- Take their fears seriously before helping them to scrutinise them.

- If you think you see them acting on a projection, or about to sabotage themselves, tell them what you see and ask if they would like to use you as a sounding board.

- Tell them what you are thinking and how you feel.

- Be consistent and trustworthy in your own actions.

Holy Virtue and Holy Idea: Courage and faith

Courage is trusting the body's and heart's intuition enough to act on them. When a car is hurtling towards you, the body does not wait for the mind to tell it what to do. Doubt questions even the instincts while trying to recreate courage through certainty. Many Sixes have a taste of the heart state of courage when, in the midst of calamitous danger, they have simply known what to do and done it. Sixes who achieve this awareness as part of their daily existence allow the immediate experience of life to affect them, and respond with caring and appropriate action.

Faith is not belief, nor can it be created by proof. Sixes look to the world to provide evidence they can place faith in it, and one negative can cancel years' worth of positive signals. When a projection has the kind of force and believability engendered by a fearful mind, it is hard for Sixes to realise they are looking for something outside to explain the sense of threat that may only exist within, a result of their habit of mind.

By practising trust, initially as an act of will, Sixes reach the inner state of faith where they simply focus on a truthful positive experience without automatically questioning its truth or looking for the hidden negative. They, like Shakespeare's valiant, 'taste of death but once', for they realise that they can utterly trust that they are sustained by life.

Faith is the understanding that, as creation is one thing and fundamentally 'works', it can be utterly trusted, it sustains and provides: the Divine will 'come through' for us. The **courageous** heart has discovered its own true nature and trusts itself and its movements within the world.

Chapter 8

Type Seven
The Optimist

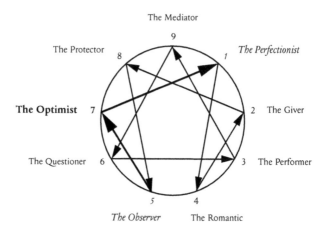

Outward appearance

Type Sevens are the eternal optimists of the Enneagram, fear types who appear the opposite of fearful. They tend to be cheerful, energetic, charming, gregarious and imaginative. Workaholics whose focus is on the fun of the project not the goal, have difficulty completing projects, with many simultaneous interests and options, and, intolerant of pain, they can appear superficial to more serious types.

Life seems to be experienced as a vast playground with the Seven at the centre, sampling all its pleasures. They enjoy sharing enjoyment and put energy into making people feel good, but can also seem self-centred. When painful experiences approach, they move away, either physically or into the pleasures of imagination. If pushed to acknowledge pain, they attempt to rationalise it away.

> *'If I'm feeling a lot of heavy negative energy coming at me, the first place I go is inside to work out a way of getting out of this feeling, whatever it may be – change it, or show how the glass is actually half full, not half empty.'*

Sevens like to have many options open to them in work as well as leisure. They are natural networkers and often have many jobs. Their way of thinking is global and they enjoy bringing apparently unrelated ideas and people together to create a new synthesis.

> *'I'm a general practitioner; I also do occupational therapy. I have a lot of hobbies and I'm reading all the time, six or seven books at a time. I do the bookkeeping for my husband's business. Then I do my "volunteer" work. And now I'm interested in adjunctive work like guided imagery for patients, so I've started a certification course in that.'*

Dreaming up and initiating something is fun for Sevens, especially if it involves others, but their imagination is so powerful that once started it feels already complete: *'So why bother with the drudgery of actually doing it? After all, I've already had the experience.'* Focused on the process not the result, if a project looks about to fail, they easily move the goalposts, or move to a new project, whilst explaining how the apparent failure was really an advantage.

Having many options allows them loopholes for escape if they start to feel trapped, and they can seem elusive. They see themselves as reliable, yet may double- or treble-book themselves because of their many interests.

Hating to feel limited in anything, they do things their own way *'in my own good time'*, and rationalise their actions or reframe the terms of a commitment to avoid pain, humiliation or boredom, not realising that others may feel let down or betrayed.

> *'I can rationalise anything. I've done things in the past that weren't that honourable. I'd rationalise it: it won't hurt anyone; the other guy was the real crook; or, I deserve that — that's a big one, I really do deserve the best in life.'*

Sevens are self-referent and can be narcissistic. Though they enjoy their friends, their attention is on their own needs and pleasures, and they are out of touch with their deeper emotions.

> *'I don't want to be seen as shallow. I don't think I am. But. . . it's not that I don't feel deeply, but I don't want to show it. I get underrated and misunderstood a lot. But in general it's fine because I'm busy all the time.'*

Faced with another's problems, they want to solve them as soon as possible so life can be happy again.

> *'Mr Fix It applies to me — it just makes sense, the impulse is to fix it to solve the problem. It's physical, like I want to jump up and do it. Why would you tell me your problem if you don't want it fixed — I mean, I wouldn't tell you my problems.'*

Sevens see themselves, like life, as full of possibilities, able to excel at anything they turn their hands to and entitled to the best.

> *'Well, my ideas and interests are so great. If he wants to talk to me, he has to grab my attention. I'll just go off into what I'm interested in. If I get that it is important to him, I have to be really polite and force myself to listen.'*

Unaware Sevens can be self-centred, grabbing, mendacious and hypocritical seekers of pleasure, easily bored and ruthless in their quest to experience everything. They can also be unfocused, rebellious and self-destructive.

Aware Sevens can be enthusiastic, perceptive, generous, creative and caring, able to use their vivid and far-ranging imagination, powers of synthesis and love of people to support individuals and causes of worldwide importance.

Inner concerns and childhood scenarios

Sevens kept hurt at bay in a frightening world by using their imagination to create pleasant options that distanced them from pain. When a situation became painful, they learnt to pay just enough attention not to get in trouble, while focusing almost entirely on inner vistas of wonderful possibilities.

> *'If I'm bored or anxious, I just go away. I look as though I'm still interested, but my attention is elsewhere. Just now I was outside that window, imagining what's going on over there, what I like to do when it's sunny, people I like to do it with, and what I'll do later. It's real and absorbing.'*

They also learnt to glamorise the present when it was good, to make it even more exciting, and remember the past selectively. Sevens do not usually report an unhappy childhood.

> *'My memory of the past is a rerun of all the happy family films my father took – the little girl running around and having a great time – though talking to people who were there then, I know that's not true.'*

Narcissism and pleasure became unconscious camouflage for their fear of being judged, rejected or humiliated, and, as adults, of having their positive self-image punctured.

> *'From a very early age, I shut off my feelings in order to survive. Recently, I've remembered that some tremendous emotional traumas occurred, and I blocked out this feeling. I did not want to feel this pain again, the abandonment, the separation, the lack of love, the humiliation, that I felt as a child.'*

Passion and Fixation: Gluttony and planning

Gluttony is the emotional habit that keeps fear at bay by focusing on the myriad enjoyable possibilities. Sevens do not pick one good thing and experience it in all its depth, but sample a little of all the best available.

> *'It's in everything I do, the most mundane. For example, I like lots of textures and different flavours in my food. New projects – ah, the potential – this one will be the one – until it takes too much effort and the next one comes along. My ultimate goal is to experience everything.'*

Often gluttony masks anxiety about deep-felt emotion. Sevens want to move on, get out of the situation and not feel it. Along with this desire goes an ability not shared by other types to 'switch off' the negative, and not knowing others can't, they can perceive other types as wallowing in negative emotions.

> *'When something bad happens to me, I immediately find a whole lot of ways to divert my attention and get busy and get out of it. Non-action or hanging around wallowing in emotion is, if I'm truthful, frightening, though what I think is "What's the point, we've felt it, let's get on with life now."'*

Moving from one experience to another, and living in the mind where there are no limits to what can be experienced, can make Sevens, for all their charm, inaccessible. *'I'm not present most of the time – I'm off in the future, and it's very pleasant there. Why should I come back?'*

Planning as a mental preoccupation is not a matter of to-do lists, though as Sevens mature they may well write lists to help them keep track of essentials. Sevens' attention is on how they will experience everything they want, and to make a step-by-step plan and stick to it is both too limiting and allows no space for manoeuvre. They say it is fun to plan, whether or not the plans are carried out, often finding more fun in planning than doing. It is a way of being open to all possibilities.

> *'It's a kind of rolling plan – a bit like one of those architect's drawing boards that you can move forward or back – and it includes all the possible options, my whole life. Whenever something changes, I just update the plan. It does include goals, but there can be many ways of getting there. The goals don't change, but the means do, and the goals can be moved forward or back, depending...'*

Planning is a way of avoiding pain, and is intensified as soon as anything threatening happens. *'Any projected anxiety about the future and then the mind starts racing...'*

Since the plan is all-encompassing, Sevens identify with it. Seemingly spontaneous, they can unexpectedly balk if a new idea or unexpected threat to the plan comes in.

> *'We nearly split up when my wife kept criticising one of my business ventures. I couldn't get that it was the plan, not me, she was attacking – and it did feel like an attack. All she was trying to do was warn me she had a gut feeling it would turn out a waste of time and money. She didn't know I felt as though she was questioning my whole validity as a human being.'*

Stress

> *'No matter what I do, I still keep getting hemmed in by [limitations, deadlines, etc.].'*

Sevens encounter stress when firm boundaries appear – for example, inescapable deadlines in work or emotional confrontations. The fear of criticism and the fear of making mistakes that are normal, if unconscious, aspects of the Seven become intensified and conscious as they take on aspects of Type One, the Perfectionist. They become irritable, nit-picking, angry at anything that seems to interfere or censure them, self-critical, and their standards become very high.

> 'It's painful. It's frightening. Everything becomes very urgent, like it should have happened already, and I get really angry because it hasn't. I lash out at anyone who gets too close – it's the ones I love most that I hurt most. And I kick and shout at furniture – it gets in my way, it should have been elsewhere. But I do get a lot of energy and things do get done – they have to.'

Security

In emotional security, Sevens take on aspects of the Observer, Type Five. They are happy to spend time alone with a good book, and withdraw somewhat from relationships. They may not actively seek time alone, but are satisfied to take a more background role than usual. In intimate relationships, this stance can cause problems, since withdrawal may be read as rejection, and Sevens' discomfort with deep feelings is accentuated in emotional security. Hating boundaries imposed by others, they become fearful when their own emotional boundaries start to crumble.

> 'It can be uncomfortable when things get too intimate and close in one-on-one relationships – it's fear of the discomfort if things get too gooey and deep – what do I do with this? Sexually, it's easy, but in the emotions it's not easy, specially staying with it for a long time. It's ironic that the closer I get to someone, the more I just want to watch TV with them.'

Subtypes

The Passion of gluttony is primarily about avoiding fear and pain by maintaining the sense that 'There is nothing to fear – fear is meaningless – I am free and entitled to experience all the good that life has to offer'.

Dissipating the raw energy and obscuring gluttony from everyday consciousness, the subtype allows Sevens not to have to face the possibility of encountering limitation, lack or fear in a threatening world.

Self-preservation: Family/like-minded defenders

Gluttony can be expressed even while personal survival is the main imperative by forming a 'family' of like-minded people, who provide varied and exciting input, and who can be trusted to back the Seven up if their safety is threatened, and vice versa.

> *'I've loads of friends, all over – some abroad – and each one of them is necessary to me, even if I don't see them that often. I've always had this village in my mind where one day we're all going to live happily ever after. It's very detailed, all the plans and everything, who's going to live where, what trees and plants... I hate to admit to myself it'll never happen.'*

Social: Sacrifice/martyr

Social subtype Sevens often appear more serious and anxious than other Sevens, even to the extent that others doubt they are Sevens. Their attention goes to the happiness of the group, and they are able to sacrifice their own immediate happiness for the group's well-being, whether that is their family, their team or the world. They can sometimes even look like Type One, as of course it's not possible to save the world, so if the world is their focus, they are often in stress, and self-criticism can play a big part in their make-up.

'I don't like it but I can put up with it. It will be wonderful, so if I have to do something right now that I don't really want to, to ensure it, then I will. If it goes on for too long, I'm told I moan about it. I have to give myself rewards – like a piece of software that I absolutely must have, right now. But I do beat myself up about not doing enough sometimes.'

Sexual: Fascination / suggestibility

In one-to-one relating, gluttony manifests as intense and immediate fascination with new people and the possibilities they represent. Sevens' attention focuses minutely on the new person or idea, to the exclusion of anything else; whilst this is happening, they are suggestible to the interests of the person, even when they've never considered them before.

'Of course I wanted to go scuba diving – right now! I knew nothing about it, but I wasn't going to say so. I know I can do anything I turn my hand to, so it was bound to be fine – and fun!'

Sevens glamorise people, and their interest is so intense the person may be deeply shocked when they become fascinated by something else and move on.

'There I was in a hot tub with my wife on one side and this gorgeous interesting actress from Los Angeles on the other, who was obviously interested in me. We got talking, and it flashed through my mind what fun it would be to go back to LA with her... And she would have my babies... I could see them... I mean, I did seriously consider it for a moment.'

Relationships

Sevens place a lot of value on friendships and family. Although the life of the mind is stimulating, real experiences with real people are much more satisfying. Unconsciously, having many and varied relationships confirms their idea of themselves as exciting people.

Relationships are based on shared pleasures. Friends and partners can be hurt when Sevens move away from pain, or frustrated when they try to 'fix' their friends' pain. Empathy has to be learned by narcissists if they realise they want their relationship(s) to deepen.

> *'I can get into someone else's joy a lot easier than I can get into their pain. Sometimes I have to literally leave the room because I cannot be with that pain. It's not because I feel for her in her pain, but because it triggers my own.'*

Sevens can be loyal, supportive and stimulating partners, offering access to things others might not ordinarily experience, once they have sorted out their own priorities. Their feeling of entitlement makes it hard for them to believe one person could be enough for them.

> *'Later on in life I had to realise that I was not quite as great as my mother had told me I was; I had to be taken down a few notches in order to sustain a relationship.'*

Unconsciously, they also find it hard to trust that anyone loves them enough to commit fully to them.

> *'Once you have forgiven me a few times, I start to believe that you really will be there for me, and I feel safe to be with you – and maybe, eventually, start to touch the pain that I secretly know I'm always running away from.'*

They may be quite able to rationalise multiple partners, since each one is unique and does not affect the way they feel about the other(s). The commitment of marriage can be seen as *'such a completely and utterly stupid idea that I had to do it for the experience'*. Once committed, however, they can stay for a lifetime.

'I don't even think of long-term relationship. We're just together. It's like making it new all the time; I don't look at her from the past. She's a really good friend – my best playmate, I suppose. Is it really 30 years? I never thought of it in those terms. Also she's the most sexually exciting person I've ever been with. That's not the only thing, but it helps keep it interesting.'

Things Sevens can do to help themselves grow

- Take up a meditation practice; notice the boredom factor in personal growth (been there, done that) and stay steady with it.

- Beware the 'flight into light' – seeing yourself as enlightened and beyond pain now that you are involved in growth.

- Realise that pleasure is only half the story: remind yourself you may be missing something and include painful experiences.

- Notice your mind racing and reaching for options: slow down and focus on the present moment whether pleasant or painful; ask yourself what you are avoiding.

- Let go of some of the options: a deeper focus on fewer things may bring you more valuable experiences.

- Notice that when you limit your options you feel as though nothing will ever happen, and it's all pointless: remind yourself this isn't true.

- Notice yourself rationalising and reframing, particularly when criticised or pinned down: ask yourself what the facts are.

- Use your anger as a signal to listen to what the other person is saying and consider its validity; ask yourself what you are avoiding.

- Learn to include criticism and conflict.

- Practise doing, and completing, one thing at a time.

- Practise restraining your impulse to 'fix' problems so that everyone can feel good.

- Notice how you discount people who might make you feel or look inferior (even if they were friends yesterday), and feel superior to those who don't have your energy and optimism; ask yourself, 'Am I really so wonderful?'

Things friends can do to support Sevens

- Support them in all of the above.

- Help them to stay in the present by asking how they feel.

- Point out reframes and rationalisations in a non-critical way.

- Point out that when they are 'racing' they might be running away from something.

- Make your own thoughts, feelings and needs important.

- Help them to value other people and focus outside themselves.

- Create an environment in which it is safe for them to explore and express pain.

- Help them recognise what they are missing by focusing on pleasure alone.

Holy Virtue and Holy Idea:
Sobriety and holy work

Sobriety is a state of being in which the emotions are focused and single-pointed, and is also called constancy. Sevens look for fullness by sampling as much as possible of what the world offers. As they grow, they realise that a complete experience is only available within themselves, with the deep and committed focus of the heart on what is truly worthwhile, and what is actually present.

Their internal plan, covering all possible routes to satisfaction, masks the fact that a sense of purpose, and willingness to go deep and complete that purpose, are what bring satisfaction. **Holy work** is the equivalent in the mental realm of sobriety, allowing Sevens to transcend their fear of pain and enter deeply into the state that T. S. Eliot called 'the condition of complete simplicity costing not less than everything'. It is not an ideation, or a mental choice of a worthwhile job, but an experience of joyful necessity. Sevens discover that rather than the earnestness implied by the words, the experience of constancy symbolised by these words generates immense gratitude for the genuine richness of life lived in the present, fully engaged and committed.

Holy work is the realisation that work (engagement) in the present is sacred work, that now is where the unfolding perfection of creation can be known as assured, and participated in. **Sobriety** enters into and wholly inhabits the world it finds itself in, giving and receiving in true measure.

Chapter 9

Type Eight

The Protector

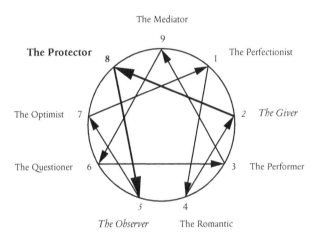

The Mediator

9

The Protector 8

1 The Perfectionist

The Optimist 7

2 *The Giver*

The Questioner 6

3 The Performer

5 4

The Observer The Romantic

Outward appearance

Type Eights are usually energetic, intense, bossy, rebellious, protective, dogmatic, all-or-nothing people who work hard, play hard and often take charge of any enterprise they are involved in, from a trip to the pub to an international business deal.

To others they may seem aggressive, but this is not usually how they see themselves, and they are often unaware of their impact, saying they are simply being direct. They have very personal ethics, involving integrity, truth and justice, through which they view the world as either/or. They are often dogmatic – *'I may be in error but I'm never in doubt'* – and though they value fairness can be slow to hear another viewpoint.

Their response to situations is immediate, and most, though not all, are easily angry; on the other hand, often when they appear angry to others they feel they are simply expressing themselves passionately. People who meet their directness with evasion, half-truths and rationalisation, or seem to withhold information, will be confronted. Eights demand truth and a clear resolution.

> *'I don't want to provoke others to fear, or to fighting out of fear. I don't really understand how other people react so negatively – my intention isn't to damage but to get clear.'*

Eights trust people who match their energy, and become focused and supportive when an issue is in the open. Others may be surprised to find that if they fight back they are liked, and that once an argument is over the anger is forgotten.

They appear to act on impulse most of the time. With a low boredom threshold, they are usually very active, but some can sit around 'doing nothing' for days or months, on the basis that *'if there's nothing worth doing, why do anything?'*

Passionate, and excessive in everything that feels life-enhancing or important to them, they are the last to leave a party they are enjoying, but also the last to leave work if they have committed to a goal. If they see it as worthwhile, they immerse themselves and keep going till exhausted. If life is quiet, they either turn to something else or increase their own energy to get things moving.

> *'I "be provocative" without even thinking of it and take up people's space without necessarily being aware of it – it's just that I feel something and it needs to be expressed, and I don't think of the impact or the consequences.'*

Eights seem to want to control. They take centre stage, are persistent in pursuing issues and seem only to be happy directing things. They have an intuitive sense of power: where it lies, whether they are threatened, and how to take or regain control. This is not always as clear-cut as it seems, as in fact they seek not to be the controller, but not to be controlled, and would often prefer not to have to take charge.

> *'It really isn't that I have to dominate, though I suppose some Eights are like that, but I refuse to be controlled. "They" ain't going to get me! And I walk away as often as I fight. If I don't care about the issue or respect the person, I can't be bothered.'*

It is not so obvious that they also control themselves. Most say they feel they are holding back constantly lest their energy and emotions overwhelm them and others. Big things that matter may take time to get under way, and anger towards people who matter may be displaced or suppressed until the pressure is so great it is forced out, often explosively.

Eights' vulnerability is hidden from themselves as well as others. Trusting their gut feelings, they can be naive and deeply hurt by betrayal. They test people's trustworthiness, usually unconsciously, by raising painful issues or making cutting remarks.

> *'Slights that are really hurtful just seem to come out and I don't know where they've come from. I didn't even notice them till my wife pointed it out. Sometimes I've cracked a joke only to be told I hurt someone.'*

Having to be strong to survive, they do not allow themselves to admit what they need, and if they do, *'it is so hard to ask that it may come out like a demand because it has so much power behind it'*. Eights also find it hard to express their truest thoughts and feelings, and when they try to, wanting to tell the truth and be understood, it may take a long conversation before they feel they have really painted a complete picture.

Eights are extremely protective and supportive of friends and loved ones, and can fight hard on behalf of anyone treated unjustly who is not strong enough to fight for themselves. Powerful people, most of them enjoy empowering others.

Unaware Eights can be cynics, bullies, law breakers and strong-arm people, unaware of others' feelings and using force, lies, manipulation or violence to get their own way.

Aware Eights can be deeply loving, protective and empowering, using their great energy and natural authority to combat injustice in the home and in society.

Inner concerns and childhood scenarios

Eights decided that to survive in an unjust, threatening and often violent world they needed to be stronger than anyone else. It seemed that the strong were valued, got what they wanted and remained unhurt, while the weak were despised and damaged.

> *'I remember the moment I realised consciously it was me and them. I was 12, John Kennedy had just been shot...and I knew it was a set-up. Whatever we know of him now, in those days he was the hero who would end apartheid and change the world. I thought, "If they can kill him, they can kill anyone. So, the bad guys are really in charge. They can do what they want." But not to me. I won't let them get me.'*

Most remember being dominated mentally or physically. Often the child who expressed the family's rage, they may have taken on the role of protector of siblings, or of one parent against another or the world. Most were overtly rebellious, though some simply became uncooperative and secretly contemptuous.

To stay strong, Eights adopted a habit of internal denial that protected them from awareness of their own vulnerability, and the needs that strong people do not have.

> 'When I'm denying, I don't know about it. I have become conscious of denying softer emotions, higher-order needs like being nurtured or helped, treated in a certain way. I can run in circles with no idea I'm needing something, or acting defensively, and it's hard even to hear it from another.'

It also protects Eights from the devastating knowledge that their focus of attention produces in them the very behaviour they hate in others: domination, insensitivity and injustice.

Although Eights are self-referencing – they act on their own rather than others' opinions – they are also 'self-forgetters'. Denial is a facet of self-forgetting, in which Eights replace their essential goals with the energetic pursuit of enjoyment, helping friends, or goals that are not their own.

Passion and Fixation: Lust and vengeance

Eights' emotional focus of **lust** is not just (or even at all) sexual but an urgent impulsive reaching out to grasp life fully: lust for life. Focusing on whatever makes them feel fully alive, they may bring as much gusto to intellectual or spiritual pursuits as to 'bed, booze and board'.

> 'I want a lot, and I don't understand people who are frightened – come on, it's good. I do overdo it – once you start it's hard to stop. Zero to 100 is easy, but cruising at 55 is hard. I can get excessive about diets too – it's good for me and I just go for it – while I do!'

Their great capacity for sensate experience also defuses their energy and releases the strain of constant control, and is one of the ways of self-forgetting.

> *'I've a great capacity for not getting the essential things done, or even little things like putting up a shelf – I'd much rather do some gardening or whatever. Hanging out with good friends is about the best – well, second-best.'*

Lust can become grasping if it looks as though the normally generous Eight might miss out – even down to hiding the last bit of the special cheese.

Vengeance focuses on injustice and redressing the balance. Seeing the world in black and white, believing themselves right, Eights assign blame and direct the force of their anger towards righting the wrong. Unlike Ones, this is not about 'the rules': for an Eight, each judgement is circumstantial: *'I didn't want to have to send her to jail – the world's a better place without her husband.'*

They will ensure the punishment fits the crime, and can go to great lengths to do so. Even with friends, *'I want them to admit they were wrong and make them change their ways.'* If anger is conscious and expressed, issues can be resolved and forgotten, whereas if unconscious or suppressed it can become obsessive.

> *'My father was a military man, domineering and violent. I will never, ever, ever lose my temper. There's nothing it's worth getting angry about. But in honesty I must admit…how I got someone sacked without appearing to be involved, how righteous I felt when someone got their comeuppance…'*

If Eights discover they have violated their own principles, possibly by harming someone, they can blame themselves deeply and their vengeance is turned against themselves. The black-or-white approach is turned inwards – *'If I'm not good, then I must be wholly bad'* – and in private they may experience pain that others would never suspect.

Stress

> *'No matter what I do, I still feel controlled by [events, that person...] (or I still feel out of control/overpowered).'*

When not in control of circumstances, weak or in self-vengeance, Eights take on aspects of the Five, the Observer, withdrawing mentally or physically to think things through and regain balance. Some disappear into compulsive activities such as reading or playing patience. In extreme situations this can last months, and they become depressed, inactive, incommunicative and unable to decide what they think and act on it.

> *'I started getting really tense – there wasn't a room in this house that was my room. I got severely depressed and slept all the time, wouldn't answer the phone... I felt all the levels of control were out of my hands.'*

Security

In the security of a trusted relationship, Eights become more Two-like (the Giver). Much more compliant, giving and easily affected, they admit things matter to them. Their protective and empowering instincts are magnified, and they enjoy their increased openness. However, it brings insecurities, including fear that it won't work out, and they may retreat into the aggressive approach after a while, with the feeling, *'What about my needs? Get off my back...'*

> *'When we got married, I started getting all these terrifying fantasies that she would die in a storm or something. It's the first time I've ever thought that way, I always thought other people were crazy to have those thoughts. What happens to her matters. Now I've really opened myself up. And then when you have a baby, you've really opened yourself up to things totally beyond your control.'*

Subtypes

The Passion of lust is often called 'excess' because it drives an all-or-nothing approach to life. As belly types, Eights are self-forgetters, and lust for life counters vulnerability and affirms 'I am', when total attention is engaged in whatever feels good, right or necessary right now. This can be anything from physical pleasure to righting a wrong, fighting a cause, intellectual pursuits or enjoying fine art. Seemingly paradoxically, it also extends to painful emotions and spiritual practice: the point is that if it's worth having, *'I want it all, and now!'*

Dissipating the raw energy and obscuring lust from everyday consciousness, the subtype allows Eights not to have to face the pain of forgetfulness of being, the feeling that they 'are not' that underlies lust.

Self-preservation: Satisfactory survival

In the area of personal survival, Eights will ensure they have what they need to survive in a satisfactory way. They may buy things in bulk, or hoard, or be compulsive about having enough of the right kind of food available at the right time. It covers all aspects of a 'satisfactory' life.

> *'All my friends were starting to retire early and I thought it would be nice if we could, maybe fairly soon if I worked hard enough. So I went to a financial adviser, and he looked at my assets, and then he looked at me with a sort of disbelieving laugh, and said, "How much exactly do you think you need, to have the life you say you want?"'*

Social: Friendship

Eights manifest lust in the social arena by having many friends, often a network of friends who work and/or play together. They like to introduce friends to each other, make sure everyone enjoys life, and provide mutual support and protection in times of need.

> *'It's just really nice to have lots of friends. I'm usually at the centre of the group, or the one who organises what we do, but that's not the point. Of course I want to have a good time, and I will, but even more I want them to. I organise parties and invite friends who wouldn't normally meet – a biker and a banker, say – and really enjoy their surprise that they get on with each other.'*

Sexual: Possession/surrender

Eights who prefer relating one-to-one have 'their' special friends, felt to be lifetime relationships. Possessiveness may not be obvious, but they need to know they are central to a person's life. They look for someone whom they can trust enough to surrender to and let go of control, and with the surrender they become very vulnerable to betrayal.

> *'I've had to realise I don't need to know every single thing that goes on in his head. But it used to upset me to hear him telling other people things he hadn't told me – like, "Sure, you can talk to other women, I'm not jealous, but you damn well better not give them a part of you that you haven't given me." Surrender is very insidious. There's a level on which I just want to let go and not have to be in control all the time, and that easily turns into "If you love me, look after me." Ugh!'*

Relationships

Although Eights value friendship deeply, a few find it hard to achieve because of their need for control, and their dogmatism.

> *'In a lot of ways I've had to give up on control in order to have any kind of a relationship. I've realised that something is only*

an issue for my type, so I don't have the right to lay down the law.'

Working relationships can be tricky because of the power issues involved, and Eights do not tolerate being bossed unless they respect and believe in their boss. They want to be able to trust and count on friends and partners.

'Predictability – not changing the rules once you've let me know what they are for you. Don't change plans. Talk to me when I need you to. Back what you say – do it. Integrity is important – if you bend the rules without discussing them with me first, it feels like betrayal.'

As belly types, they feel the need of connection, and some of their aggressive behaviour is an attempt to get other people to connect with them.

'One of the worst things in the world is being ignored – it's almost intolerable to have that sense of separation. You walk away and I'll come forward to make sure it's all right.'

Independent and pleasure-loving, they may see commitment as a trap, but once committed in friendship or love, they are loyal for life, though it may not be conventional since they have their own rules. Usually, Eights are unaware of trying to have things their way.

'Neither of us saw ourselves as controlling. But when he's still shaving and I'm all revved up and ready to go – grrr! So then I'll go and have a cigarette and won't be rushed.'

Fighting is almost essential for an Eight in relationship: it clears the air, gets things straight and is, for them, an exciting way of making contact safely. It is vital for a partner to know when to fight back and when not: Eights can be talked out of it if the issue is unimportant.

> *'Fighting is important – it may feel destructive to you initially, but actually it's for clarification, out of love not malice. I will not go to sleep with an issue unresolved. The one time he said to me "Go to bed, you'll feel different in the morning" and I actually tried it, I woke up in exactly the same state of rage.'*

Eights can be enlivening and interesting partners: *'Married to [an Eight] I may be delighted, provoked and horrified, but I'm never bored.'* They can also be tirelessly protective, and supportive of their partner's self-fulfilment.

> *'I know she's intelligent and capable, and I love it, but going out into the world – any threat of danger – it's important she comes with me so I know she's safe. It looks like control but it's to protect her.'*

Partners should be aware that Eights, maybe disconcertingly, need support too. When they start to show how deeply they can hurt, they trust enough to truly receive love.

Things Eights can do to help themselves grow

- Take up a meditation practice, and stay with it when your impulse is to get up and go.

- Take time during the day to check how your energy is and whether you are acting on impulse.

- Use anger to remind you to relax and breathe deeply several times a day.

- Check out your impact with your friends and colleagues: are you being too much?

- Before moving into action, review the possible consequences, and remember long-term goals.

- Practise delaying stimulation and gratification, and learn to accept boredom and fear.

- When you feel bored and about to go into action, ask yourself if you are suppressing fear or sadness, and learn to let yourself feel them.

- Start to recognise and welcome your vulnerability and weaknesses as a sign of innocence.

- In confrontations, make sure you listen to the other side, and use it as an opportunity to recognise the validity of other points of view.

- Ask friends and colleagues for a clear statement of rules, and notice when the impulse to break rules is for the hell of it rather than from an appropriate response to a situation.

- Start to question whether excessive behaviours (socialising and so on) are a way of concealing and forgetting your real priorities.

- Write down and review insights about yourself daily as a way of opposing self-forgetfulness and denial.

- Notice your tendency to blame others, and acknowledge your involvement in negative situations.

Things friends can do to support Eights

- Encourage them in all of the above.

- Be encouraging rather than telling them what they are doing wrong, or they will simply think, 'That's bad? Well, watch this!'

- Let them know when they are being intimidating or hurtful in the things they say.

- Be straightforward and forthright, and fight with them if need be in the spirit of clarification, not of winning.

- Remind them their truth is not necessarily the full or real truth.

Holy Virtue and Holy Idea: Innocence and truth

Innocence is a state of being in which the world is experienced as safe, without hidden intent, and in which an Eight also is innocent of agendas or defences. In innocence it is possible to respond to life appropriately in each moment through the bodily 'knowing' of what is right, without the need to judge or consciously evaluate. Eights realise that their grasping for experiences is an attempt to recreate the essential experience of life force flowing through them fully and rightly at every moment.

Allowing and welcoming life as it is leads Eights to realise that **truth** is not either/or but the totality of existence as it is. Any set of facts, or any concept, however right, is not necessarily true. In essence, there is only one truth, which cannot be arrived at or recreated by seeking justice, and truth changes continually without ever changing its nature. Eights learn moderation, above all through knowing that 'the truth which can be spoken is not the truth'.

Truth is the realisation that all of creation simply *is*, that God is all-that-is and that in reality there is no separation of the divine from existence. The **innocent** heart receives each moment as it truly is without memory, judgement or expectation; finding itself in divine flow, it responds freshly to what is.

Chapter 10

Type Nine
The Mediator

The Mediator

Outward appearance
=================

Outward appearance

Type Nines are usually warm, friendly, tolerant, accommodating and uncompetitive, and enjoy being with others. They prefer a peaceful, structured, predictable and comfortable life, and like to have a sense of belonging. Even when their lifestyle looks unpredictable, harmony is deeply important, and they will often unconsciously set up small rituals (yoga at 7, coffee at 4) to give structure to an otherwise unstructured day. They find it hard to know their own priorities, and go along with other people's wishes, sometimes even taking on their accent, vocabulary and body language.

They are often very active, having many interests and hobbies and putting a considerable amount of energy into their work. They prefer to be with people, and are most productive on behalf of others or in a team. Socially, they can appear laid-back and mellow, but they have a lot of latent energy and can swing between high activity and exhausted or lethargic inactivity.

> *'If I'm left on my own, often I feel lonely and depressed. There's a "juice" in being with other people and I'll seek that out. I often feel I should pay my clients rather than the other way round because it gives me structure. They walk into my office and I kind of take on – it's very intuitive and immediate – their values and beliefs, even their mannerisms. Being able to use my skills to help them gives me a sense of solidity, and there's a lot of power and good feeling, whereas on my own it's very difficult.'*

Nines are 'self-forgetting' and lose awareness of what is essentially important to them. They are easily distracted even when alone and leave high personal priorities till last. This looks like procrastination but is not intentional. Self-forgetting is literally a 'forgetting' of 'who I am', and unconsciously it's as though they do not have permission to pay attention to what actually matters to them personally. Unimportant tasks, new interests, other people – all seem more immediate than the essential work, both material and spiritual. They meet deadlines at the last minute and often rely on other people to remind them.

> *'It's the classic scenario: I'll be going upstairs to fetch my diary, then the plants call me and I go to water them, but the sink needs to be cleaned… An hour later it's "What did I come up*

> *here for?" I have a lot of goals but it's hard to focus. People keep having to remind me to do things for myself, like keep appointments.'*

Nines see all points of view and, when seeking or giving information, like to have the whole context and all relevant information stated. Therefore they can seem long-winded or pedantic and find it hard to come to decisions. They seem to sit on the fence most of the time.

> *'Do I have all the information here? I'm not sure what I think, particularly if I've got several people giving different opinions. In business meetings I sit and listen, and every argument has something valid in it.'*

Since their world seems so fluid, Nines want to feel in control and can be obsessive about details. They accumulate information as well as things and can get deeply involved in making plans which may never materialise. Absorbed in something that to onlookers seems secondary, they can be distant and lose interest in other matters. At the same time, they want others to participate or at least acknowledge their project.

Nines are not good at fighting their own battles, though they will fight for others fiercely as arbitrators or to ensure one side is not overlooked. In personal matters they find it hard to know what they think or feel. Anger is expressed passively in stubbornness or inaction, or in outbursts so distant in time from the original source that even they are not sure what it's about.

They dislike being told what to do, but will do nothing rather than disagree, until the 'flow' takes them elsewhere.

> *'I wake up one day and say, "No, this isn't me," and everyone says, "Hey, I thought you were on the team." Well, it never really fit, but I was there and I might as well do it, but now it's not it any more and it's time to move on.'*

Unaware Nines can be needy, indecisive, judgemental, apathetic and obsessive, craving relationships yet blaming the world for their situation and expressing it through complaint and passive-aggressive behaviour.

Aware Nines can be empathic and generous, peaceful to be with, open-minded, forgiving, and able to create harmony by intuitively sensing the appropriate balance of energy in a group and bringing out each person's real contribution. Intuitively, they will know the right thing to do and take action without hesitation.

Inner concerns and childhood scenarios

Nines wished to retain their intuitive feeling of connection and belonging in a world that seemed to be one of separation and lovelessness, or where the love was directed elsewhere. They learnt to submerge themselves, put their attention outward and merge with others.

They report that in childhood they were not heard, their family seeming to overlook them. To take a stance, positive or negative, and so draw attention to themselves would have been to risk further separation. It seemed preferable to forget themselves and be what other people seemed to expect. This could lead to adults seeing them either as so amenable that they did not need any attention paid to them or as someone without much character or talent. Nines often report being seen as 'not particularly bright'.

> *'For years it was insinuated I was clumsy and stupid and it was as though I had to be that. I would just space out. It was only in my twenties I decided I possibly had some intelligence, and started to study – and did very well.'*

Some were actively told not to express themselves.

> *'It was very clearly "Don't talk about what you're feeling" – or even seeing. Since it was not acknowledged, I just decided that I had no opinion.'*

They also learnt to 'forget' their anger at not being seen and displace their considerable natural energy into inessentials lest it force them to act. Their anger was expressed in ways that seemed not to involve a stance on their part.

> *'Holding out is a way of getting even and expressing anger passively. When they needed or wanted me, I just wasn't present (mentally, not physically) – it drove them crazy – then, of course, they got angry, so it's not my anger that's being expressed.'*

Passion and Fixation: Sloth and indolence

Sloth and indolence are inwardly focused, not outwardly, and support self-forgetting. The emotional focus of **sloth** keeps Nines disconnected from their own emotions, particularly the physical impulse of anger. They replace them with a gut-level awareness of others' moods and feelings, which is so immediate it is as though they 'become' the other person whilst in their presence.

Nines can break through sloth by discovering their anger, but usually they feel *'it's not worth it; who am I to be angry at this, I'm not sure I even am angry'*, especially in the actual presence of someone who angers them. If acknowledged, it will probably be volcanic, and displaced: *'I'm not sure what I'm angry about but I am angry – and you may have something to do with it.'*

If they feel pushed to make a firm statement about their own wishes or boundaries – that is, to remember themselves – anger rises, which they can disown by blaming someone else for forcing them to be angry.

'It feels like driving with both feet down – one on the accelerator and one on the brake – it's very frustrating. And there's an internal rage which I can't say and often don't feel, but other people do, and ask me if I'm angry and it's "No, but I will be if you keep asking."'

Activity may stop when Nines start to question their self-forgetting and search for who they are apart from *'an echo and reflection of other people'*. In the initial dilemma of looking inside and seeming to find no one, at risk of losing identity whether self-forgetting or waking up, they can feel impotent and aimless.

Inertia is also part of the mental preoccupation of **indolence**. It is a form of self-neglect in which, caught between things that have to be done or unable to decide which of their many personal priorities to pursue, they cannot motivate themselves to choose and act on their choice. Nines are indolent towards their essential priorities to the extent that they often say they have not planned to be where they are in life – *'It just sort of happened.'*

'I need a structure to keep me on track and usually that's provided by another person because I even find it difficult to do that for myself. The temptation is to find an interesting structure and just go with that.'

They also 'space out', burdened not only by the many things they could do, and wish to do, and need to do because there's a backlog of postponed activities, but by their very way of paying attention. Wishing to include everything, they can think about many different things at once, and self-forgetting makes it hard to prioritise even thoughts.

'I think a lot – but actually it's a sort of rumination, with the same thoughts going round and round, over and over again. I don't seem to get anywhere.'

When with others, what someone looks like, their feelings, their ideas and what they are saying are all overlaid on Nines' existing thoughts, and rather than focus on one they distance themselves mentally.

Nines avoid acknowledging sloth and indolence, and cut off the enormous physical energy that threatens to overwhelm them by 'narcotising' – numbing their awareness with repetitive and almost compulsive inessential activities. This can be as simple as reading or computer games, but may be anything that helps them to forget the pain of forgetting.

Stress

> *'No matter what I do, I don't feel in harmony with/at one with/included with/belonging to that [those] person [people].'*

Under stress, when being pushed or forced by circumstance to take a position, Nines take on aspects of Type Six, Questioner. They become fearful, aware of all potential threats, and either withdrawn and even more compliant, or obdurate, more stubborn and belligerent. Procrastination increases as their indecision turns to doubt, and it can seem that the only safety lies in refusing to act at all.

> *'Taking action means I've got to put myself out there and take a position, and that is dangerous. I used to think I was a Six, because I was fearful for most of my childhood. My father was determined we should be articulate, and we used to have debates on topical subjects at the dinner table and I always lost – but we weren't allowed to talk about anything that was actually going on in the family.'*

Fear is often focused on issues of not belonging, other people's intentions and doubts about their position in relation to others, rather than on the more generalised 'worst-case scenario' of the true Six.

Security

When emotionally secure, feeling at home, included and appreciated, Nines become more Three-like (the Performer). Their energy becomes directed and they can achieve many things excellently in a short time. The Three tendency to seek approval adds to their natural wish to do what others want, and a supportive relationship with a partner or a boss brings out their enthusiasm and abilities.

> 'I've never worked so hard or so successfully before. I adore my wife and our baby, and it's motivated me to get everything done around the house at last – but also my clients say they've noticed a difference. Maybe it's because the quicker I work, the more time I get at home?'

Subtypes

The Passion of sloth was originally named 'accidie', described by Aquinas as 'turning one's back on things, through depression or self-hatred; a torpor of spirit which prevents one from getting down to anything good'. Many Nines recognise this very poignantly, as they are far from 'slothful' by the modern definition. Sloth requires a Nine to 'forget' her or his very self, to be asleep to being.

Dissipating the raw energy and obscuring sloth from everyday consciousness, the subtype allows Nines to remain comfortably unaware they have lost touch with the essence of their individual existence.

Self-preservation: Appetite

By compulsively immersing themselves in some form of numbing behaviour, Nines avoid having to take action from their own choice. It also keeps the world at bay, minimising the dual risks of separation (through having to take a stance) and of losing identity (by having to merge with people).

*'I used to watch TV whenever I wasn't doing something else...
It was always on at my parents' house so the family didn't have
to interact. I remember once a close friend came round who
was having a very difficult time and I just watched videos for
the whole day. I could find something "interesting" in anything,
from the most frivolous to the driest subject.'*

Social: Participation

Social Nines channel self-forgetting and physical energy into
merging with the group. Participation may mean joining
teams, or setting up activity groups for others to participate
in, or networking. Nines act on behalf of the group to the
extent that they lose themselves, though such action feels
'right' and therefore 'chosen'.

*'We are all one. It's really important to me that everyone joins
in and that the whole group works together, and that we enjoy
ourselves doing it. I will take the lead in the group if a fight is
taking place, and I love creating harmony. Conflict really is an
illusion – if only everyone could get that!'*

Sexual: Union

These Nines have a passionate drive to find the person with
whom they can merge completely, feeling thereby they will
find themselves. It can also be channelled into religion and
the desire to be one with God. In this case there may be a
conflict between merging with the partner or with God, or
they look for the divine in the partner and merge with that.
'I *am* you' gives the illusion of being a self.

*'There is simply a big gap between me and the absolute love
I long for. If I could only find that and sink myself into it
completely, then everything would be all right; I would
be whole.'*

Relationships

Nines are so attuned to other people they can be mistaken for heart types. Supportive relationships are very important, allowing them to relax and just 'be' without having to take responsibility, and giving them their motivation to act.

> *'For me it's finding the person who has a sense of life and wanting to be somewhere, that will help take me there with them – the ability to draw me into action when I'm having trouble moving.'*

Nines will not deny people even if they are feeling intruded upon. Friends can be frustrated by their compliance – *'I've heard it's hard to be with me because I don't know right away what I want'* – and by their tacit demand to be included and listened to. Nines may be surprised when friends notice their suppressed anger and encourage them to express it.

> *'Often contacting anger is a way of focusing my attention: when that's the case, I've noticed people don't see it as threatening.'*

Though Nines seek union in intimacy they may avoid commitment, or if in a relationship fail to disengage once it's over, because either would mean taking a position and getting off the fence. Some move from relationship to relationship as they merge with the wishes of each new partner.

However, once in a partnership, Nines do not think of leaving and are committed to a settled and inseparable relationship. They can support and celebrate their partner's success without jealousy or competition, finding it exciting to cheer another on and see them fulfil their potential. They are loyal and generous, and able to respond to their partner's needs as they arise.

It is in intimacy that their anger is most likely to emerge. Partners who also want intimacy, want to help Nines discover their own identity, because when they are merged they disappear. It can feel like relating to a cloud, and when partners ask for something more definite, they may find the Nine backs off.

> *'I spent a lot of time not knowing what I felt, pretty blank; even when I looked really hard I didn't know – so she's had to project on to me what she thought I felt. So we would be at loggerheads a lot of the time, which I didn't like, but it actually helps to trigger me into finding out what I want. But most of the time I hate it. Leave me alone to find out what I want – and when I have, you can help me.'*

Fighting in relationship is a way of creating separation so Nines can have a sense of their own identity, and is therefore also a way of making contact and creating intimacy in the meeting of two equal individuals.

Things Nines can do to help themselves grow

- Start a daily practice of previewing what is important for you today, and reviewing how well you did with this.

- Start a practice or join a group that encourages you to contact and express your gut feelings in the moment, including anger.

- Notice when you get distracted or obsessive, what the accompanying feelings were/are, and start to let yourself feel them through.

- Avoid belittling yourself and making others more important or more intelligent.

- Notice yourself deciding to agree or disagree: ask yourself what you think, regardless of their opinion.

- Notice how your thoughts go away from yourself: take the time to ask yourself what is important to you.

- Decide on goals, make action plans with clear time frames and enlist support in sticking to them.

- Notice how dependency and merging allow you to blame others when things go wrong.

- Notice your stubbornness and passive resistance, and start to state what you disagree with.

- Use anger and passive aggression as cues to look back and see what was important to you that you missed: where did the anger originate?

- Express anger in your imagination, to blow off the charge of the backlog and make it more immediate.

- Notice your discomfort around change and start to welcome it anyway.

- Practise taking a position and stating it – even if to start with it seems arbitrary or as though you are acting.

- Learn to say no to others' requests.

Things friends can do to support Nines

- Encourage them in all of the above.

- Help them keep focused by bringing their attention back, but gently; otherwise, they will simply shut down.

- Provide a supportive environment for them to experience and explore anger.

- Help them differentiate between positive expression of their position and anger by telling them which feels like which to you.

- Ask them what they want and need, what is important to them.

Holy Virtue and Holy Idea:
Right action and love

As Nines bring their attention back inside, they find a source of great energy and intuitive wisdom in their belly-based awareness. Instead of looking for the motivation for action outside themselves, they understand that it lies within. Instead of turning their attention to inessentials to disguise their fear of separation, they realise they are innately connected to all that is, and from that springs the ability to know, and carry out, the **right action** in any moment.

This goes hand in hand with the awareness of **love**. In the grip of their fixation, Nines believe that to be an 'I' means to be separate, and to merge with another is to achieve the supreme one-ness. They must be indolent towards their true selves to achieve merger. This is a spiritual trap, since to be at one is actually to experience the underlying unity of two (or more) separate entities. Love is a state in which the awareness opens to include all others, and in this experience the Nine realises they do not need to deny or suppress themselves since they are already fundamentally inseparable and loved in return.

Love is the understanding that reality is love, its function is benevolent, and all that exists is a part of this infinite manifestation of love. **Right action** is the natural expression of a being in harmony with reality and in tune with their own and Creation's energy.

Chapter 11

Seeing Below
the Surface
Types That Look Alike

It may be hard at first to decide which type you are. Maybe two or even more of the types seem familiar. Nines, for example, can often identify with all types. Occasionally, people have found, after years of thinking they were one type, they were actually another. It may take a skilled Enneagram teacher over an hour of careful interviewing to discover a person's type, and even then they ensure the person confirms it from their own understanding.

Whichever centre we 'live in' – head, heart or belly – we have the capacity to feel all human emotion, though maybe not as frequently or as intensely as our own centre's default emotion. Similarly, our personal backgrounds predispose us to have certain beliefs, issues, preferences and ways of acting in day-to-day situations that do not necessarily 'match' our type.

People of different types may act, or even think and feel, in similar ways. Fear of flying does not make one a Six, any more than a concern for justice belongs only to the Eight; nor is it only the Three who can work hard, long hours to achieve something.

Ways in which a person of one type may 'look like' another

'True' type look-alikes

There are particular types that can appear very similar on the surface. The most obvious of these are:

- One and Six (anxious)
- One and Eight (angry, righteous)
- Two and Seven (playful, optimistic, many activities)
- Two and Nine (other people's needs)
- Three and Seven (workaholic, pleasing)
- Three and Eight (workaholic, determined)
- Eight and counter-phobic Six (confronting).

Stress and security

We all take on a flavour of another type when in stress or security. It is possible to spend so long in one of these states that we start to act and feel like that type. For example, a person whose childhood was very stressful may, as an adult, behave in some ways very like their stress type; or in a long-term secure and happy relationship, we may 'become' our security type for a while.

Wings

We may have a particularly strong link to one of our wing points, either permanently or from time to time. For example, when I first met the Enneagram I was sure I was a Nine, because some of my behaviour is very Nine-like (but also because I secretly thought Nines were 'nicer people' than Eights). It took feedback from a close friend, and some honesty, to know that I am an Eight. I can still look Nine-like, though.

Cultural influences

This is too large a topic for this book and can only be described in terms of general, and vague, tendencies. However, there can sometimes be a cultural overlay on people's behaviour which may blur their true type. For example, the USA values Type Three attributes (go get it), though in recent years Type Six (political paranoia) has been seen; the UK historically has taught its children Type Five (stiff upper lip) with a touch of Eight (John Bull). Some cultures still have strong male/female stereotyping, even when their members are brought up in other countries. The most obvious are Type Two as the ideal for female behaviour, and Types Eight, Three or One for males.

Stress and security as aids to determining type

Although stress and security behaviours may produce a temporary look-alike, they are also a very great help in differentiating true look-alikes. Always use them as a check to decide and confirm your type. For example, One and Four are quite strong look-alikes, yet in security and stress they change in very different ways – so different that it should be possible to see clearly which is the core type. Refer to the chapter on each type for more information when using stress and security in this way.

So which type am I?

The following tables will help you once you have narrowed down the choice to two or three possible types, by asking simple questions to elicit the focus of attention behind similar behaviours. They are not a definitive questionnaire to establish which of all the nine possible types you are. So far no such questionnaire exists (since type is defined by a hidden focus of attention very difficult to translate into behavioural questions), though there are a number of tests available.

The only sure way of knowing your type is through self-observation, and from the unmistakable sense of affinity with others of your type when you hear them talk about themselves – and the surprising contrast with other types. This is why I recommend Narrative Tradition workshops as an essential next step in working with the Enneagram.

Using the tables

The tables contain, for each pair of types, a statement of which sort of look-alike they are, brief descriptions of how they look alike, and two or three questions. The questions are baldly stated, to help you answer a clear 'yes' or 'no'. Always give a definite answer, even when it's a case of 'more often than not'. If you dislike a phrase or think 'I don't know', it may be genuinely irrelevant to you, or it might be there is a part of your personality you would rather not admit to.

If you use these questions to help type other people, please don't ask them the questions out of the blue and then *tell* them what they are. Have them read the book if they are interested, and ask them what they think: only they can know themselves well enough to decide for sure.

To avoid repetition I have listed the possible common characteristics, with the distinguishing questions, under the first look-alike type of the two, and therefore there is no table for Nines.

Examples:

If you think you may be a	Six		
or an	Eight:	look at Type Six for	Six vs Eight

If you think you may be a	Two		
or a	Three or a Seven:	look at Type Two for	Two vs Three
		and	Two vs Seven
		then	
		look at Type Three for	Three vs Seven

It is a good idea to cover the right-hand columns at first, so your answers to the questions are spontaneous.

Type One: The Perfectionist

Two: Wing look-alike

	One	Two
Two with One wing: self-righteous, self-critical, perfectionist.		
One with Two wing: concern for others/altruism.		
Is it more important to make the other person involved happy than to complete a task correctly?	N	Y
Do you tend to present different facets of yourself to different people?	N	Y

Three: Possible look-alike

	One	Three
Workaholic, active, competent, motivate others, apparently self-confident.		
Are you willing to cut corners to get the job done?	N	Y
Is excellence in the detail more important than success?	Y	N

Four: Security/stress look-alike

	One	Four
Intense, melancholy, yearning, see what's wrong/ missing, critical, self-deprecating, idealistic.	One	Four
Stressed Ones: emotional.		
Secure Fours: critical.		
Is your criticality more about ethics and correct behaviour…	Y	N
…or about relationship and personal issues?	N	Y
Would completing a task properly usually take priority over sorting out a problem in a relationship?	Y	N

Five: Possible look-alike

	One	Five
Knowledgeable, controlled energy, physical tension, get things right, emotions private.	One	Five
Are you more likely to be irritated than frightened if someone shouts at you?	Y	N
Do you nearly always need time alone to consider your opinion?	N	Y

Six: Common look-alike

	One	Six
Procrastinating, anxious, distrustful of authority, self-doubting, want to get it right, fairness/ morality issues, support causes, think things out, possibly argumentative, seem critical.	One	Six
Do you nearly always have an angry and critical inner voice with standards that you could never live up to?	Y	N
When you reach a point of view do you tend to question it again?	N	Y

Seven: Security/stress look-alike

Angry under pressure, arrogant.	One	Seven
Stressed Sevens: critical of self and others, irritable, nit-picking.		
Secure Ones: may be playful, adventurous, pleasure-loving.		
Are irritation and self-criticality a constant feature in your life?	Y	N
Are you in general optimistic about the future?	N	Y

Eight: Common look-alike

Moralistic, black-and-white view, judgemental, angry, take charge, do things 'my way', concerned about fairness/justice, desire truth.	One	Eight
Do you generally abide by a set of fixed rules about behaviour?	Y	N
Is it easy for you to allow yourself pleasure, and follow pleasant circumstances through to the end?	N	Y

Nine: Wing look-alike

Procrastinating, unexpected anger.	One	Nine
Nine with One wing: precise, self-critical, judging.		
One with Nine wing: desire harmony, can 'slob out'.		
Do you find it easy to hold your own position in a discussion?	Y	N
Would you say harmonious relations come before doing the right thing?	N	Y

Type Two: The Giver

THREE: WING LOOK-ALIKE

	Two	Three
Change to please, need approval, don't know inner needs, image conscious.	Two	Three
Two with Three wing: task-oriented, particularly on behalf of a chosen boss/mentor.		
Three with Two wing (particularly in the caring professions and house-wives/husbands): successfully take on role of giver.		
Do you gain the greatest approval from pleasing others…	Y	N
…or from getting the job done?	N	Y
Do you get emotional if you feel people are making continuous demands without giving anything back?	Y	N

FOUR: SECURITY/STRESS LOOK-ALIKE

	Two	Four
Emotional, empathic, seek approval/connection, can seem vain/special, feel empty, change to please.	Two	Four
Secure Twos: more emotional, maybe nostalgic or insecure, more artistic.		
Stressed Fours: meet others' needs.		
Is your focus generally on yourself and your emotions?	N	Y
In a good relationship, do you feel sure of your ability to please the other, and therefore in control of it?	Y	N

FIVE: VERY UNLIKELY LOOK-ALIKE

	Two	Five
Information-gathering, not knowing own feelings in the moment. Twos able to be unobtrusive and intellectual.	Two	Five
Do you use your knowledge to help you please others?	Y	N

Six: Possible look-alike with self-preservation subtype of Six

	Two	Six
Self-preservation Sixes: warm, pleasant, want to serve, go toward others, need to be liked.		
Twos: anxious, fearful of making mistakes or doing the wrong thing.		
Are you more attracted to powerful interesting people...	Y	N
...or to underdog causes?	N	Y
Are you generally suspicious about people's hidden motives?	N	Y

Seven: Common look-alike

	Two	Seven
Energetic, optimistic, friendly, want to be liked, value relationships, charming, seductive, like to have fun and ensure others have fun, selective in whom they approach, hard-working, sometimes seen as shallow.		
Is it important to you to meet other people's needs before your own?	Y	N
Can you easily get absorbed in your own intellectual interests if alone?	N	Y

Eight: Security/stress look-alike

	Two	Eight
Generous, energetic, pleasure-loving, have difficulty receiving, gregarious, drawn to power, can be strong leaders.		
Stressed Twos: may become angry, push for what they want.		
Secure Eights: more generous and intuitively giving.		
How do you deal with someone being angry with you – do you easily fight back?	N	Y
Are you nearly always concerned with others' approval, even if you disagree with them?	Y	N

NINE: COMMON LOOK-ALIKE

	Two	Nine
Intuitive of others' feelings and needs, put those needs first, take on the flavour of others (merge), helpful, generous, unaware of own needs/priorities, want to be liked, may feel unappreciated or not noticed, active.		
Do you move actively towards selected people you are interested in…	Y	N
…or do you find yourself responding to (merging with) most people around you?	N	Y
Is your basic motivation to actively give pleasure to others…	Y	N
…or not to rock the boat?	N	Y

Type Three: The Performer

FOUR: WING LOOK-ALIKE

	Three	Four
Competitive, concerned with image, charming.		
Three with Four wing: may lean to artistic expression, experience sadness particularly in relationships.		
Four with Three wing: prefers the higher to the sadder emotions, energetic, career-oriented.		
Do you find it quite easy to empathise with other people's painful emotions?	N	Y
Do you instinctively change the way you are to meet what you think other people will like?	Y	N

FIVE: NOT A LOOK-ALIKE

Six: Security/stress look-alike

Loyal, back causes, self-doubting, hard-working.	Three	Six
Secure Threes: may become anxious, doubt themselves and their ability to succeed.		
Stressed Sixes: can focus on goals and handle success.		
Do you feel it's important that people like you and that you can easily get along with anyone if you want to?	Y	N
Are you anxious about a lot of things, even if they don't relate to your potential success or failure?	N	Y

Seven: Common look-alike

Energetic, workaholic, set goals, make lists and plans, feel they can achieve, able to make themselves liked, avoid negative feelings.	Three	Seven
Do you find yourself keeping your options open, even if it means moving the goalposts?	N	Y
In a fairly long-term project, is your attention on ensuring its success…	Y	N
…or can you become bored before the end and move to something more interesting?	N	Y

Eight: Common look-alike

Energetic, workaholic, leadership and control issues, can-do attitude, like winning, can inadvertently step on others in pursuit of goal, frustrated by incompetence.	Three	Eight
If someone confronts you angrily, and in your view wrongly, about something you have done, is your instinct to fight about it?	N	Y
Would you change your stance or stated point of view because doing so would help you achieve a goal?	Y	N

NINE: SECURITY/STRESS: UNLIKELY LOOK-ALIKE

	Three	Nine
Stressed Threes: can be swayed in their opinion, more likely to go along with others' agendas and wishes.		
Secure Nines: can be energetic and efficient achievers, feeling they know what they want.		
When you are with good friends, is it likely to be just as enjoyable, if not more, if there is no specific activity planned?	N	Y
Is it very important to be seen as successful in your chosen field?	Y	N

Type Four: The Romantic

FIVE: WING LOOK-ALIKE

	Four	Five
Feel unworthy of attention, may seem arrogant or unapproachable.		
Four with Five wing: aloof/shy, need privacy, may be out of touch with or suppressing emotions.		
Five with Four wing: artistic, flamboyant, may have a strong inner emotional life tending to melancholy.		
Is the life of the mind most important and nourishing to you...	N	Y
...or would you say you experience life more through feelings?	Y	N
When you are with other people, do you sometimes feel ashamed, even if there is no obvious reason for it?	Y	N

Six: Possible look-alike
with counter-phobic Six

	Four	Six
Break rules, excited by danger, hate to be told what to do, anti-authoritarian, fearful, self-doubting, idealistic.	Four	Six
Are you attracted to deep emotions, in yourself or others?	Y	N
Do you tend to look to the future, thinking about what might go wrong and how to avert it?	N	Y

Seven: Possible look-alike

	Four	Seven
Special, intense, stylish, reckless, apparent push–pull in relationship (there, then not there), self-referencing.	Four	Seven
Do you prefer to avoid suffering if possible, and, if not, heal or move on from it quickly?	N	Y
Do you have a sense that you have been or might be abandoned by people you love?	Y	N

Eight: Possible look-alike

	Four	Eight
Intense, emotional, reckless, high standards, value authenticity, flamboyant, vulnerable heart, self-referencing.	Four	Eight
Can a 'good row' with someone you care for leave you feeling energised and more sure of the relationship?	N	Y
Does it seem natural to dwell on and explore your emotions at some depth and over time?	Y	N

Nine: Possible look-alike

Melancholy, self-deprecating, want to be understood, feel they don't belong or different, immersed in relationship, spaced out, experience self as loving, seek connection. Depressed Four can be slothful.	Four	Nine
Do you sometimes wonder if you as an individual exist for other people, that no one notices or listens to you, or that you bore them?	N	Y
When a relationship becomes close, do you find yourself noticing and criticising imperfections in your partner, even if yesterday they were perfect for you?	Y	N

Type Five: The Observer

Six: Wing look-alike

Five with Six wing: may be aware of fear and other Six issues, may question own reality.	Five	Six
Six with Five wing: withdrawn, private, contemplative.		
Are you aware of a pretty immediate reaction to events, even if you may not voice it straight away?	N	Y
Does it often seem to you that life is like watching a film, nothing is very close to you when it happens?	Y	N

Seven: Security/stress look-alike

Wide-ranging imagination and love of ideas.	Five	Seven
Stressed Fives: dislike committing themselves, scan for all possible options to escape threat, may seem evasive or scattered.		
Secure Sevens: may enjoy solitary intellectual pursuits, sit back and observe rather than being the focal point, may seem withdrawn.		
When you consider all available options, are most of them pleasant or leading to a pleasant outcome?	N	Y
Do you start to feel drained or over-extended unless you have at least part of each day to yourself?	Y	N

EIGHT: SECURITY/STRESS LOOK-ALIKE

	Five	Eight
Secure Fives: more outgoing, even bossy, may access anger, may be protective of loved ones.	Five	Eight
Stressed Eights: withdraw physically or mentally, need space to re-group and think, may aggressively shut out the world.		
If confronted, can you access your own anger easily and immediately, even if you don't express it?	N	Y
Do you become fearful if you feel intruded upon or threatened?	Y	N

NINE: POSSIBLE LOOK-ALIKE

	Five	Nine
Liking privacy, observing from a distance, delaying action, stubborn, withdrawing, accumulating information.	Five	Nine
Do you have a clear sense of your own boundaries, and find it easy to maintain them?	Y	N
Do you find yourself going along with other people and their wishes, even when you feel you need to be alone?	N	Y

Type Six: The Questioner
SEVEN: WING LOOK-ALIKE

	Six	Seven
Imaginative, fear-based.	Six	Seven
Six with Seven wing: can be fun-loving and gregarious, like multiple activities, networkers.		
Seven with Six wing: may be aware of fears or anxiety, more likely to plan for negative as well as positive outcomes.		
Do you find your imagination mostly takes you to pleasant future possibilities and/or bright ideals?	N	Y
When you succeed at something do you find it easy to believe the compliments you receive?	N	Y

EIGHT: COMMON LOOK-ALIKE WITH COUNTER-PHOBIC SIX

	Six	Eight
Confrontational, dislike rules, have authority issues, fight for causes, see the world as hostile or potentially unfriendly, do dangerous things.		
If need be, do you find it easy and enjoyable to take on a leadership role?	N	Y
Do you frequently question your own decisions, even after you think you have made up your mind?	Y	N

NINE: SECURITY/STRESS LOOK-ALIKE

	Six	Nine
Secure Sixes: lose the sense of threat, enjoy simply being with people and allow them in.		
Stressed Nines: may be very fearful, mistrust others, see future pessimistically, expect harm.		
Do you tend to visualise specific threats and worst possible outcomes in most situations?	Y	N
Do you more often than not allow people to affect you, rather than keeping yourself safely uninvolved?	N	Y

Type Seven: The Optimist
EIGHT: WING LOOK-ALIKE

	Seven	Eight
Energetic, direct in pursuit of goal, enjoy consuming, pleasure-loving, angry when challenged.		
Would you more easily 'go around the houses', plan and manoeuvre, sometimes deviously, to get what you want, than fight for it?	Y	N
If someone is angry about something you have done, is your first reaction to fight back (even if quietly and reasonably)…	N	Y
…or explain the situation and disarm them?	Y	N

NINE: POSSIBLE LOOK-ALIKE

	Seven	Nine
Pleasure-loving, avoid conflict, get side-tracked, have many interests.		
Do you usually know what you want?	Y	N
Are you more concerned with or interested in what other people feel and want than your own intentions?	N	Y

Type Eight: The Protector

NINE: WING LOOK-ALIKE

	Eight	Nine
Stubborn, postpone own priorities, pleasure-seeking, misplaced anger, narcotising.		
Do you usually have a clear point of view which it is easy for you to defend?	Y	N
Do you nearly always submerge or forget your own wishes for the sake of maintaining harmony?	N	Y

Chapter 12

Communication
Using the Enneagram to Create Understanding

Everyone has experienced misunderstandings in relationships. Some people just don't seem to grasp our point of view, or sometimes even hear what we say. Others hold views that must be mistaken; it's hard to believe they actually mean what they seem to say.

Once we grasp how fundamentally the world views of the types differ, we start to realise that an opinion or feeling that seems self-evident from where we stand may *truly* seem crazy to someone else, and vice versa. It is as though we speak different languages without realising it. The words are the same, so we believe we can understand and be understood, while in truth we may be far from it.

Whenever I hear the phrase 'But doesn't everybody...?' I know we're on to an aspect of type; and in workshops, when a participant says that, much to their shock the response is usually a chorus of 'Er – no.'

Unless we are talking to someone of our own type, and sometimes even then, probably only part of our message is getting across. Other types simply hear the words we use in a different context. Not only that, each type has different energy, different body language and a different way of approaching people.

The Enneagram is not a way of matching people to people or to jobs. It predicts that if two people meet on the diagram at some point, they may understand that part of each other's behaviour better (whether they like it or not is not important). In life, however, people of the same type or of apparently opposed types may hate or love each other; and although each type has certain talents, an employer may be surprised by which type is actually doing the job well.

J. Krishnamurti (1895–1986), internationally renowned philosopher and spiritual teacher, rightly said that understanding creates compassion; it also fosters creative relationships. If we want to be understood, and in turn to understand, we must get into the skins of others and see life as they see it. By learning the languages of the other types, suspending our own judgements on what they say and how they come across, we discover understanding and heal relationships.

This chapter contains simple lists of a few communication tips for each type: what to watch out for if you *are* that type, and also if you are *talking to* that type. These tips are about day-to-day interactions, not about growth as such. Be flexible in how you apply them, and expect some 'Aha!'s along the way.

First, a few general guidelines:

- These are only tips, not rules: if an approach doesn't work, drop it!

- Don't label people or treat them as a type: they are themselves, not a type.

- If you think you know their type, try a few of these ideas and see how they respond. Remember, not everyone has all the 'typical' reactions.

- Above all, ask questions – and acknowledge the answers as valid whether they fit your own view or not. After all, they are, to the other person.

- Use communication to discover more about the different types, and why they respond as they do – including your own.

Type One: The Perfectionist
If you are a Type One

- When you have helpful input to give, make sure you acknowledge what is working before suggesting improvements.

- Praise others when they do or say something you like: they may not know you noticed.

- Beware of sarcasm or cynicism when you are feeling hurt or disrespected.

- Speak about your feelings as well as what you think: your logical approach may seem unfeeling or critical to others.

- Remember that when you are controlling or blaming yourself, you may come across as angry, so try to talk about how you feel.

- If you like someone, tell them: sometimes your self-criticism makes you seem unapproachable, so they may not be sure that you do, and may keep their distance even if they also like you.

- If others seem unhappy or dissatisfied, remember that it is probably not aimed at you, nor your responsibility, so simply listen to their troubles.

If you are talking to a Type One

- Remember they may not be aware of how they feel, so ask questions in a non-critical way to help them access their feelings.

- Don't take their angry energy personally: it may be about something completely different, and even they may not know what.

- Present your point of view as logic rather than feeling: Ones will be able to consider a new idea and take it on if it fits logically.

- Be direct: they are sensitive to, and critical of, manipulation.

- Tell them when you see something wrong, and apologise for your own mistakes and criticisms: it's reassuring to them that they are not the only ones.

- If they don't listen, invite them to tell you what they are thinking.

- Encourage them to share gentle humour and see the bright side.

Type Two: The Giver
If you are a Type Two

- Remember to tell people about yourself as well as inviting them to tell you about them.

- Try to be yourself in conversation, rather than pleasing the other person.

- If you feel taken for granted or treated unfairly, say so calmly as soon as possible.

- Ask for what you need rather than blaming others for not giving to you: not everyone has your intuition for what people need.

- Avoid the tendency to make statements about the person you're with as a roundabout way of asking for feedback: ask directly.

- Let others say no to your offers of help, without feeling rejected and offering something else instead.

- Give people space to solve their own problems.

- Allow others to give you help, instead of saying 'No, I'm fine,' and even if you genuinely don't need help, receive the offer gracefully (you may have a tendency to snap or be brusque!).

If you are talking to a Type Two

- Tell them you appreciate what they do for you.

- Let them know they don't have to be a certain way or help you for you to like them.

- If you turn them down in any way, tell them why, including your feelings, so they know they can help you best by not helping you.

- If you want to do something for them, tell them it gives you pleasure too.

- Invite them to tell you about themselves: they will tend to focus only on you.

- Ask them how they are feeling, and what they need right now, particularly if they seem emotional, spaced out or 'speedy'.

- Don't be frustrated if they don't know how they feel or turn the conversation round to you; simply let them know you are interested in them.

- Be sincere and direct: they are very sensitive to manipulation and insincerity and will shut you out if they sense it.

- At work or in a project, don't put them on their own: make sure communication lines are open.

Type Three: The Performer
If you are a Type Three

- Remember, many others are genuinely not as ambitious as you: make the effort to listen and to recognise their strong points.

- Notice if you are steamrolling others: tell them how you feel, and consider what they have to say carefully.

- Remember that you are easily distracted visually, so in important conversations place yourself where it can't happen.

- Let people know what you are truly feeling: they may like you better, not worse, for it.

- Let people know you appreciate what they contribute, at work and with friends.

- Make time to listen to people's feelings, especially loved ones.

- If you hear yourself coming back with a quick answer or solution, stop and consider what you are feeling, and communicate it.

If you are talking to a Type Three

- Criticism will only force them to 'perform' harder.

- If you want them to change how they are doing something, or consider a change, show them how it will help them achieve a better result.

- Remember, if you labour a point, they will switch off.

- To make positive contact, match their energy level: once they are with you, you can alter the pace somewhat.

- If you feel manipulated or steamrolled, let them know what it feels like: they may genuinely not know they are doing it, and they do not like hurting people.

- Don't take it personally if they get distracted or move on quickly to the next action: ask if they could slow down for a moment, and tell them why.

- Tell them if you like them and enjoy their company: they don't find it easy to believe they are valued for themselves.

Type Four: The Romantic

If you are a Type Four

- Remember, most people are not as attuned to feelings as you are.

- Tell people what you're feeling, rather than waiting for them to guess to prove they're empathic to you.

- In discussions, beware getting caught up in your emotional response.

- Try to stay focused in the here and now.

- If necessary, tell people you may seem over-emotional or distracted, and ask them to help you stay grounded.

- Invite people to help you lighten up if you feel yourself getting attached to your emotions. That includes the joyous emotions!

- Beware of being sarcastic if you feel inferior or victimised: instead, tell people what you are feeling and ask them how they see the situation.

If you are talking to a Type Four

- Match intensity with them so they feel you're there for them: if they feel you understand them, you will be able to change the pace so you are comfortable too.

- Be straightforward when asking for help – they may appear self-absorbed but will be happy to help you.

- Let them know your feeling responses as well as what you think.

- Remember that their emotions are real, even if you think they are overblown, so don't try to talk them out of them.

- Acknowledge their feelings, even in a reasoned discussion.

- Ask them what they are feeling if you feel they are 'in a mood'.

- Give them compliments, particularly for their creativity and unique contribution, rather than for their results.

- Listen to their intuitions – they may well see things you don't.

- Remember they have low self-esteem, even if it doesn't show, so let them know you care for and value them.

Type Five: The Observer
If you are a Type Five

- The more you withdraw, the more you may provoke the thing you don't want; so, if you can, tell people how you feel, even if it's only that you need space.

- Let people know that before you can make a decision you need time on your own to think it through, and that their presence interrupts your thought process.

- Let friends know that it's not that you don't have feelings; it's just that you have difficulty expressing them in the moment.

- Offer a firm time for discussions so people don't feel fobbed off.

- Let people know it's hard for you to stand your ground.

- If you feel others are demanding of you, tell them their impact on you: they may not mean it that way.

- Try to respond to people's feelings as well as words, so they don't feel rejected or dismissed.

If you are talking to a Type Five

- Be aware they are very sensitive to non-verbal signals and will withdraw if you don't seem interested and non-threatening.

- Don't take it personally if they withdraw, and remember they have difficulty expressing themselves.

- Respect their boundaries: don't cling or appear dependent.

- Tell them ahead of time if you need to talk to them.

- Give them time alone to make decisions.

- Don't over-use praise: leaving them to get on with things shows you trust them to do it well.

- Silence is not rejection – if they are there, they want to be; contact may be a smile.

- Be direct and factual; state feelings in a moderate way.

- When you ask for something, make sure it's stated as a request, not a demand.

- Remember, if they seem arrogant, aloof or irritated, it may be that they are uncomfortable.

Type Six: The Questioner

If you are a Type Six

- When you are doubting, check for the reality by asking friends what they think.

- Remember your tendency to project: when you're sure something bad is going on, ask yourself what cues you are responding to (is it something in me?) and ask others what they think and feel.

- Others may not hear the message behind your actions – remember to tell them what you feel as well as supporting them in action.

- Remember that some people actually need regular contact as proof of your reliability or friendship.

- Your doubt may be seen as untrustworthiness, because it seems you think one thing then change: tell people that you are likely to seem to vacillate, even when committed, but that if you commit to something, you will do it.

- If you catch yourself dominating a conversation, ask yourself what you feel, and consider talking about that.

If you are talking to a Type Six

- Remember, they find it hard to trust – they have a doubting mind – so don't take it personally if they seem to distrust your compliments or praise.

- Listen, and acknowledge that you understand; otherwise, you cannot be trusted.

- Be accurate and factual in what you say – remember it's easy for them to project hidden motives and meanings.

- Reassure them that you like or love them, in a non-sentimental way – action works better than words.

- Be consistent – continuity, and actions matching words, engenders trust.

- Invite them to check out their reality and help them stay out of their imagination (projections) and grounded by asking questions such as: 'Is something troubling you? What are you thinking about this situation?'

- Don't criticise or judge their fears.
- Be humorous – encourage them to laugh and see the positive side.

Type Seven: The Optimist

If you are a Type Seven

- Listen to people: their opinions and feelings may be as true as yours.
- If someone tells you a problem, ask if they would like your advice or help; don't simply tell them what they could do.
- Let people know that even implicit criticism makes you angry, and warn them not to take it personally.
- Tell friends you find it hard to speak about your feelings and what matters to you emotionally.
- Remember, you imagine things so fully that it's easy for you to believe you have told other people, when you haven't: check it out.
- When you have a brilliant idea for improving something, or you change your goalposts, let people know before you act, so they have a chance to cooperate and don't feel ignored.
- If you have delegated something to someone – at work or at home – and you have an idea for doing it even better, suggest it to them: don't rush in and do it yourself.

If you are talking to a Type Seven

- Remember that they tend to wander off in their minds; keep them present by asking questions, including their feelings.

- Engage in light-hearted conversation: participate in their enjoyment.

- Listen to and appreciate their grand visions: remember they are sharing a part of their being, and try not to invalidate their ideas.

- If you put forward an idea that may affect their plans, expect some initial resistance and give them time to incorporate it.

- Don't criticise or give instructions; make suggestions based on the short- to medium-term gain of doing things that way.

- If you feel it necessary to help them face up to a prevarication or a painful emotion: be absolutely steadfast, have stamina, and don't take it personally if they try to make you the person at fault; simply bring them back to the issue, as often as it takes.

Type Eight: The Protector

If you are a Type Eight

- Remember that a raised voice often makes other people stop listening, and that you may be louder than you think.

- If you feel unheard, rather than repeating yourself more loudly, ask the other person to help clarify the discussion by telling you what they think you have said.

- Tell people that if you ask a lot of questions, it's to understand, not to hassle them.

- Listen to other people carefully and consider their point of view before replying.

- Remember, other people don't have such immediate responses as you do: it may work to give someone time to consider rather than insisting on sorting it out *now.*

- If people hurt your feelings, tell them so at once: they may not know you can be hurt.

- Watch for your tendency to say hurtful things without meaning to, and if you do, apologise as soon as you realise it.

If you are talking to a Type Eight

- Say what you mean, ask for what you want directly, don't hedge or avoid issues: they react negatively to anything that could be manipulation.

- If you say you'll do something, do it.

- In a discussion, let them know you understand their point of view in precise terms; they will then be able to hear what you say.

- Remember, what feels like an argument or an attack to you may just be their way of engaging enjoyably and safely: tell them if it's too intense or you feel threatened.

- Tell them if you have any unspoken rules about how you want the relationship conducted, and be willing to discuss them.

- Tell them if they hurt your feelings: they may not have meant to.

- Don't tease them: they are quick to take a bait and do not easily forgive feeling humiliated.

- Don't lie unless you don't mind being attacked or written off.

Type Nine: The Mediator

If you are a Type Nine

- Remember that when you don't know what you feel or want, others may experience your silence as rejection, so tell them what is going on inside.

- Try to notice when your silence is passive resistance, and if it is, let others know where you actually stand.

- When you feel angry, say so: often you won't seem angry, just positive.

- If others ask you if you're angry, consider it rather than deny it.

- If you feel unheard, tell people that's the case rather than speaking at greater length.

- Stick to the point as much as possible.

- If you are asked a question, find out exactly what the person wants to know so you can give a focused answer.

If you are talking to a Type Nine

- Listen and let them know you have heard what is important to them.

- Acknowledge them: they often feel left out or unheard.

- Remember, when 'merging', they may seem very present, but actually may be reflecting you back: so ask questions to find out what they think.

- Remember, they can be very dispersed: ask questions to help them focus.

- When you want to know what they think or feel, don't push for answers, but create an interested space in which they can consider and decide: 'I wondered, does this fit for you? Could this be how you're feeling? I don't know but I just wondered.'

- In business meetings, remember they may agree with each speaker as they are speaking, so ask them in advance to let you know their considered opinion once the meeting is over.

Conclusion

What Do I Do Now?

How deeply you study the Enneagram is a purely personal matter. Whatever is right for you *is* right for you. If you are serious about your growth, willing to embrace the discomfort as well as the delight of self-discovery, the profound truths it reveals will provide a lifelong guide for each stage, helping you to see where you are and what to do next.

It's not prescriptive, so how you go about applying its guidance will be personal. There are so many beautiful, valid and effective ways of approaching the changes we want and need to make in ourselves, and, again, what is right for you is right for you. The Enneagram can inform and add depth to any psychological and/or spiritual path.

In my experience of over two decades working with and teaching it, there's both an interweaving – adding meaning – and a cyclical effect of introducing the Enneagram to your growth toolbox. Interweaving sharpens our understanding of the effectiveness (or not) of our practice or therapy; for some, just witnessing themselves in action as a type and letting go *becomes* the practice.

Whatever their source, genuine truths about human psychology and spirituality, and ways of approaching these, always interlock, feed into one another, 'fit'. And fit our intuitions about ourselves, what's true, what works for us, and what's not, too. As I said in Chapter 1, the proof is in the pudding: nothing is right (or wrong) for you just because someone said so. Trust your intuition, and look at the results:

do you like the taste of your pudding? Or at least the taste of what it will be once cooked? The Enneagram will help you know whether you're on the right path for you – not anyone else, *you*.

The cyclical effect is simply that the Enneagram will come and go in terms of significance and effectiveness. You may have this book on your shelves for ten years before you decide to investigate the Enneagram – and then discover that you've got the book (or many books!). Likewise, there will be times when it fades into the background, no matter how enthusiastic you were at first.

Because it's purely descriptive, there may, or probably will, come a time when you decide that you've gone as far as you can with it. I did. Then, after a while, it comes back and makes sense at a deeper level and offers new and more profound insights. If you care to accept its challenge, it does offer a lifetime of learning. This book is just a first taster.

Meanwhile, I offer a few tips.

What *not* to do next

The Enneagram, like any personality typology, can be trivialised. Though this cannot be helped, its real meaning will survive. However, even if you have decided to go no further, I hope you will read and adopt this list of what *not* to do. Some will not apply to you, but they do all apply to someone, and I can guarantee that at least one of them will pop up at some time. So please beware any temptation to:

- make it a dinner-party game, as in: 'Oh, she must be a Four – look at her hair!'

- tell people they are a certain type: not only is this rude, it can be misleading, and cause distress if they do not want to know or if you pick a type that seems 'bad' to them

- stereotype people: 'He's an Eight – he's bound to be aggressive,' 'She's a Two – you can see how manipulative she is,' and so on

- dominate people or play the guru with your superior knowledge of what they are like or what's really going on in their lives

- allow people to, or make them, feel bad about themselves because of their type: all types are as good or as bad as each other, and the Enneagram is about our highest potential, not our occasional aberrations

- use your type as an excuse for your behaviour ('I'm a Seven – I can't help double-booking people occasionally'): once you know your type, there is less excuse, not more, for some of your less loving traits.

I also invite you to point it out if you see anyone, including Enneagram teachers, doing any of these things.

Taking it further

The Enneagram is not a panacea, though simply knowing the material can bring about change in your day-to-day life. Nor does it require an all-wise teacher to help you apply it, though help may be very important at times.

It invites you to be responsible for your own life, to say, 'Now I know this about myself, and so I know how to begin to heal myself and my relationships.' In the Sufi tradition, it is seen as a God-given system which enables us to achieve 'moral healing' through our own work.

It is valuable however you use it, from simply making each day a bit happier and more of an 'Aha!' experience, to the ultimate goal of experiencing (not just believing) that we are all truly one, though our personalities seem to separate us.

With this in mind, and the fact that this is only an introductory book, I make the following suggestions. They are roughly in ascending order of intensity; it is for you to consider and apply each if and when you want to. At whatever level you do this work, there are a couple of things to remember at all times.

Befriend your personality
The goal of the Enneagram is not to overcome your personality but to befriend it and use its quirks as wake-up calls. When you see yourself locked into, or about to head into, a pattern, don't tell yourself you shouldn't, for the more you fight something, the stronger it becomes. Ask yourself why your type is being provoked and what you could do about it and learn from it.

Forgive yourself
Noticing your type in action, however 'wrong' it might sometimes seem, forgive yourself; have compassion for your personality. Don't set value judgements on your own type. Don't set yourself impossible goals of behavioural and spiritual change. The very act of seeing your patterns will start to release them.

Suggestions for deeper learning
1. Basic awareness
Follow the pointers in the chapter on your type. You may find it useful to copy them and keep them somewhere handy; in any case, look at them from time to time.

2. Self-observation

Practise self-observation or, as Gurdjieff called it, self-remembering. You might purposely stop several times a day to review what you are doing, thinking and feeling, or preview and review the day in a formal way. Alternatively – or as well – choose one aspect of your habitual pattern of behaviour or thought that you'd like to let go of. Then start catching yourself in the act when you are doing or about to do something automatic and reactive. Expect first to notice it after the event, then during, and then before you start. Soon you'll notice it's gone. This is how we drop any annoying habit, like a phrase or a physical tic, so just apply it to your type!

3. Narrative Tradition learning

Attend classes in the Narrative Tradition. This is the very best way of learning about type. Not only do you discover the many differences between people of the same type, even whilst learning more about their shared focus of attention, but you learn more about yourself in the contrast, and in the very process of describing how you manifest your own type. As Alice in Wonderland said, 'How do I know what I think, till I see what I say?' (Lewis Carroll).

4. Friends

It is very useful to have friends who know the Enneagram, to discuss what you are learning about your own and their types, experience the interaction between types in practice, and (this can be humorous as well as enlightening) give and receive feedback along the lines of 'You're Sevening again' – 'Oops, so I am.' We can't really see ourselves as others do, so actively invite feedback and ask others what their type's perspective is on events or topics.

5. Mindfulness/belly-based meditation/ contemplative prayer

These are all effectively the same thing, named by different traditions. This is a basic and essential emptying practice which helps you find the neutral ground or centre of your being, strengthens the inner observer and makes self-remembering easier on a day-to-day basis. It leads to Presence in the here and now, and forms a basis for other practices as and when they become appropriate, since it also gives us access to the safe ground within ourselves.

If you find that at this stage in your life it is too difficult, or triggers strong emotions, wait until you feel ready. Bear in mind, however, that *no one* finds it easy to begin with as type interferes and becomes very strong in the inner space as we attempt to sit in silence. We cannot fight our type's habits, but we can let them go.

You can follow the process below, or look for others with whom to practise. Nowadays there are classes and retreats almost everywhere in Zen, Vipassana, mindfulness, and contemplative and centring prayer. There are also plenty of books and websites dedicated to these and to the importance of breath to spiritual and psychological growth.

The method is simply allowing awareness to settle 'in and down' to the place in the abdomen where breath and awareness join. We relax back through our type into our centre. Sitting upright, with head erect so breath flows easily, drop into the breath that creates a pleasant feeling of fullness and relaxation against the abdominal wall, and with each breath let your awareness sink deeper to follow the movement in the abdomen that is the breath.

When type emerges in the form of thoughts, emotions or physical distractions, simply notice it and return awareness back to the breath. Do nothing but return and allow awareness to be carried, without exerting any effort

at all. If the distraction persists, then name it 'Thinking...
thinking' or 'Sensation...sensation' until it recedes. If an
emotion rises, relax right through it back to the abdominal
breath. It will vanish as well.

Simply return again and again to the breath moving in
the abdomen, and rest upon the breath. Do this for 10–
30 minutes each day, or as often as you can. At first it will
seem as though it's impossible to sit in silence without inner
distraction, but soon, if you practise, you will know where
to rest your attention when you go within, and the periods
of still centredness will become longer and deeper. Keep
practising!

6. Body work, head and heart practices, therapy

All of these can play an important part in psychological
and spiritual growth based in the Enneagram, but to discuss
them is beyond the scope of a brief introductory book. All
I'd say here is this: find what works for you and notice how
it relates to or interacts with your type; be wary of anything
that is rigid or dogmatic, for dogma stifles growth; and
know that therapy and spiritual work go hand in hand, and
at times in our lives we may need one more than the other.
So, once again, don't judge yourself. Rather, be sensitive
to your own needs as you move towards freedom from the
chains of type's automatic reactions and beliefs.

7. Direct spiritual work

There are three strands to this, all necessary.

> a. Your personal relationship with the Divine,
>   whatever that is for you, whether a personal God
>   or a sense of the greater all-that-is. Our type
>   colours this relationship, as it does between people,
>   and research shows the path to deep spiritual

awareness is different for each of the types. Only in Presence, the eternal Now, do we share the spiritual experience. Simply notice the ways in which your type interrupts your ability to be present to the Divine.

b. Working with your spiritual director, mentor, friend or teacher. Many such people now know the Enneagram, and if yours does not, it can be helpful to find one who does. This can be alongside and at infrequent intervals: I wouldn't ask anyone to drop such a crucial relationship for the sake of this model. And it may be – it often is – that you introduce the Enneagram to your spiritual director or mentor, and they embrace working with it too.

c. Retreats and workshops specifically dealing with the Enneagram in a spiritual context, and in different faith and spiritual backgrounds, can be found in many places worldwide.

Conclusion

Finally, remember growth is like climbing a staircase, not a smooth gradient, and looking ourselves in the eye can be a painful process. The personality has a vested interest in not changing – after all, you've survived all right till now, haven't you?

For everyone, there are times when we seem to be making no progress, or to be backsliding, or it seems too painful to continue looking. *These are temporary hitches.* When it happens to you, remember your highest potential, think of your goal (even when it doesn't feel real, it is), grit your teeth, weep or rage, and keep telling the truth. There is always light at the end of the tunnel, the darkest night *is* before dawn, and here is an ancient story which expresses the truth:

> *When the gods created mankind, they also created a key to the door of Heaven…and then they decided they didn't want men and women to get hold of it after all. But it was made and could not be unmade. They debated for days where they should hide it. One suggested the ocean, another deep within a mountain, another the heart of the sun. All were useless, because they knew that sooner or later people would have the skill to get to these places. Finally, the wisest of them said, 'Let us hide it in the heart of man himself. He will never look there.'*

So they did; and so it is to this day. Keep looking: the treasure is there.

FURTHER READING AND
USEFUL CONTACTS

This is not a bibliography – to list all books written on the Enneagram between the 1980s and now would occupy too many pages to warrant, and more importantly be confusing to the general reader!

Accordingly, I have confined myself to listing the best-known authors, and a few less well known whom I have found helpful and interesting. This is by no means an exhaustive list of books worth reading, merely suggestions as to where to go next. Most of the major authors have written more than one book, so unless I have found one particularly useful, I give only their first or best-known title.

Much of the material published since the early 2000s, particularly on the internet, is questionable (a Google search offers over 6.5 million hits). I come across a lot that is speculative, or written from a very personal perspective, yet communicated as though it were 'true' and validated through inquiry. I would simply suggest that if you come across anything more complex than you've found in these pages, take it with a slight pinch of salt, and test it against your inner understanding of how you really tick.

The Enneagram: Personality types

Almaas, A. H. (1998) *Facets of Unity: The Enneagram of Holy Ideas.* Berkeley: Diamond Books.

Hurley, K. and Dobson, T. (1992) *What's My Type?* San Francisco: HarperCollins.

Maitri, S. (2005) *The Enneagram of Passions and Virtues.* New York: Jeremy P. Tarcher/Penguin.

Naranjo, C. (1990) *Enneatype Structures: Self-Analysis for the Seeker.* Nevada City, CA: Gateways.

Palmer, H. (1991) *The Enneagram: Understanding Yourself and the Others in Your Life.* San Francisco: HarperCollins.

Palmer, H. (1994) *The Enneagram in Love and Work: Understanding Your Business and Intimate Relationships.* San Francisco: HarperCollins.

Riso, D. R. (1987) *Personality Types: Using the Enneagram for Self-Discovery.* Boston: Houghton Mifflin.

Rohr, R. (1990) *Discovering the Enneagram: An Ancient Tool for a New Spiritual Journey.* New York: Crossroad.

Zuercher, S. (1992) *Enneagram Spirituality: From Compulsion to Contemplation.* Notre Dame, IN: Ave Maria Press.

The Enneagram: General and esoteric

Arica perspective

No good Enneagram book could omit to reference Oscar Ichazo. However, most of what he has written on the Enneagram is not openly available: apply to the Arica Institute. Some can be found in his compilations of interviews:

Ichazo, O. (1982) *Interviews with Oscar Ichazo.* New York: Arica Institute Inc.

Additionally there has been some commentary on his trainings involving the Enneagram:

Lilly, J. (1972) *Centre of the Cyclone.* London: Bantam Press.

Lilly, J. and Hart, J. (1975) 'The Arica Training.' In C. Tart (ed.) *Transpersonal Psychologies.* San Francisco: Harper & Row.

Gurdjieff related

Bennett, J. G. (1983) *Enneagram Studies.* York Beach, ME: Samuel Weiser, Inc.

Riordan Speeth, K. (1975) 'The Gurdjieff Work.' In C. Tart (ed.) *Transpersonal Psychologies.* San Francisco: Harper & Row.

Riordan Speeth, K. (1989) *The Gurdjieff Work.* Los Angeles: Jeremy P. Tarcher.

Tart, C. (1986) *Waking Up.* Boston: Shambhala.

Walker, K. (1979) *Gurdjieff: A Study of his Teaching.* London: Unwin.

Webb, J. (1980) *The Harmonious Circle.* New York: Putnam.

Sufi

Bakhtiar, S. (1993) *God's Will Be Done: Traditional Psychoethics and Personality Paradigm.* Chicago: Kazi Publications.

Websites

The websites of some of the best-known Enneagram teachers:

Condon, T. *www.thechangeworks.com*

Hurley, K. and Donson, T. *www.hurleydonson.com*

Palmer, H. *www.enneagram.com*

Palmer, H. and Daniels, D. *www.enneagramworldwide.com*

Riso, D. R. and Hudson, R. *www.enneagraminstitute.com*

Contacts

Workshops in the Narrative Tradition, UK

Karen Webb

Enneagram Studies UK

66 Cowleigh Bank

Malvern

Worcestershire

WR14 1PH

Tel: 01684 561258

www.theenneagram.co.uk

Paul and Rosemary Cowan

The London Enneagram Centre

www.londonenneagramcentre.co.uk

Other workshops

Listings can be found in the annual *Retreats Handbook* from the Retreat Association

www.retreats.org.uk

Lightning Source UK Ltd.
Milton Keynes UK
UKOW06f0006251016

286071UK00001B/53/P